5 SECONDS
OF SUMMER

5 SECONDS OF SUMMER

THE UNAUTHORIZED BIOGRAPHY

JOE ALLAN

MICHAEL O'MARA BOOKS LIMITED

First published in Great Britain in 2014 by
Michael O'Mara Books Limited
9 Lion Yard
Tremadoc Road
London SW4 7NQ

A CIP catalogue record for this book is available from the British Library.

Papers used by Michael O'Mara Books Limited are natural, recyclable products made from wood grown in sustainable forests. The manufacturing processes conform to the environmental regulations of the country of origin.

ISBN: 978-1-78243-367-5 in hardback print format
ISBN: 978-1-78243-369-9 in trade paperback print format
ISBN: 978-1-78243-368-2 in e-book format

1 2 3 4 5 6 7 8 9 10

Designed and typeset by Design 23

Printed and bound by CPI Group (UK) Ltd, Croydon, CR0 4YY

www.mombooks.com

This book is dedicated to Tony French.
For boundless support as I took my first steps on
a hidden path.

CONTENTS

THEY CAME FROM A LAND DOWN UNDER

'We have an imaginary bus: it's called the "5SOS Bus". We're driving the bus and people come on the bus and they get off the bus, but we're the only ones who always stay on the bus. These guys aren't even best friends; they're like brothers to me now. They are like family. So wherever the band is, home is, really.'

CALUM HOOD – AUSTRALIA'S *60 MINUTES*

The Australian music scene has never been more vibrant, diverse and as rich with talent. Aside from 5 Seconds of Summer, artists as varied as Iggy Azalea, the new queen of hip-hop, singer-songwriter Vance Joy, electronic act Empire of the Sun and drum and bass stars, Pendulum, have, in recent times, achieved critical acclaim and success on a global scale.

This breakthrough has not been strictly limited to performers. In the last couple of years, singer-songwriter Sia Furler, who was born in Adelaide, has become one of the most sought-after songwriters in the world, penning international hits for a multitude of artists including Rihanna, Lea Michele, David Guetta, Rita Ora, Katy Perry and Jessie J.

It hasn't always been the case that Australian artists would find automatic, international acceptance for their music, however, and for many years much of Australia's biggest-selling home-grown talent found success outside of their homeland hard to come by. Whether it was due to a lack of an original sound, or simply the continent's geographical isolation, Australian exports were largely limited to artists who sounded very similar to their American and British counterparts, or novelty acts using their Aussie roots as a gimmick. When Australian new-wave, pop-rock group Men at Work scored a worldwide hit in early 1983 with the song 'Down Under', it appeared that they fitted squarely into the latter category. With lyrics filled with every stereotype about Australia and Australian life you could possibly imagine, and a sound that vaguely echoed the rock–reggae hybrid of Britain's The Police, Men at Work looked as though they had anything but a profound message. Yet there was more to the song than its infectious chorus, and on closer inspection it could be taken as a sly comment on the fact that Australian culture, its artists and the music the country was producing were being largely ignored, dismissed and reduced to cliché.

The cries of 'Can't you hear the thunder?' and 'You better run, you better take cover' in the chorus could have just as easily applied to the explosion of untapped talent and new music that was about to erupt from the 'land down under' over the next few years.

From the mid-eighties onwards, the Australian nation saw an unprecedented outpouring of new musical talent. There were massive international crossover artists such as rock band INXS and metal pioneers AC/DC, country singer Keith Urban, and a multitude of pop acts including Savage Garden, Holly Valance, Delta Goodrem and the undisputed princess of pop herself, Kylie Minogue. The country's vast size and apparent isolation from outside influences seemed to be no longer an issue and, if anything, only added to the creativity and uniqueness of the musicians it produced.

It was into this global music market that 5 Seconds of Summer was launched. In what is a classic rags-to-riches tale, they landed a string of worldwide hit singles, a multi-platinum-selling debut album and an army of loyal fans. Yet, while many things may have changed in the music business in the last few decades, one thing has stayed more or less the same: there is no such thing as an overnight success, and 5SOS were no exception.

Even considering today's culture of instant fame and celebrity, thanks to the likes of YouTube and reality television, in the music business, things tend to take a little longer, requiring a lot of planning and hard work behind the scenes

– not to mention finding an artist with the talent, the look and the right attitude to succeed in the first place. However, originality and aptitude have rarely been the only factors to guarantee success, and with the continuing pull of reality shows and televised singing competitions such as *The Voice, The X Factor* and *American Idol,* luck and timing have an important part to play. It's hardly surprising that the members of a manufactured pop band, such as One Direction, become global superstars so rapidly when you consider the blanket exposure they receive over a relatively short space of time. Multiple appearances on the UK's most-watched television show, *The X Factor,* every week for several months inevitably helped One Direction reach a wide and accepting audience. When you then contemplate the added global exposure for every performance across online video channels such as YouTube and other internet sites, it was almost inevitable the band would build an enormous fan base and reap the many rewards of fame.

But building a fan following from the ground up might be thought of as the easy part. Keeping those fans on board, when the 'next big thing' comes along, is much harder. These days, while fame and fortune can come very quickly, the really tricky part, and the key to true achievement, is making it last.

Around the same time as Men at Work were flying the flag for Australia, British pop band Duran Duran were making it big in America. In 1983, they were already well established back in the UK, having signed to EMI Records – former home to The Beatles and one of the biggest and most successful record companies in the world – a few years earlier. 'Hungry Like the Wolf', their breakout song in the US, was actually their fifth UK hit single, lifted from their second album, *Rio* (their self-titled debut album having gone largely unnoticed in America in 1981). Their triumphs were hard earned, but the band had the weight of a powerful press and marketing team behind them. To break America, the band was swept along on a whirlwind tour, performing endless numbers of shows, but were stuck half way around the world. A gruelling schedule for anyone, and before long it started to take its toll on some of the band members. Hardly the rapid success story enjoyed by One Direction, but the end results amounted to the same.

Duran Duran's original drummer, Roger Taylor, told *Classic Pop* magazine, 'People think it is amazing being in a successful band from the outside, but it's not the greatest world to be in – you live in hotels, need security to walk down the street, can't go to the shops. It's a difficult life.' The pressures are often unexpected and the workload extreme, he continued. 'I do see similarities with One Direction today. I worry a little bit about them because they are young like we were in an intense environment … I was nineteen years old when I joined the band, and by twenty-three I was playing Madison Square Garden, flying around the world in my own airplane. It was too much.'

Things in the music industry may have changed hugely in

the last thirty years, but it seems many of the pressures faced by new artists looking for their big breaks have remained more or less the same, and one key element of achieving (and maintaining) fame and fortune remains: you have to be prepared to work for it.

In light of their origins, One Direction's success in America could almost be taken for granted. Put together and groomed by a savvy team of music industry professionals, given massive exposure on a highly rated television series (and then via a sold-out arena tour following the show's conclusion), signed to Simon Cowell's hugely powerful record label Syco and given a debut single created by a team of producers responsible for some of the biggest hits by artists such as Britney Spears, Westlife, Justin Bieber and Demi Lovato – how could they lose?

What *is* truly remarkable is when a singer or band comes along with no prior connections to the music industry, and with little more than a dream to create and share the music they love, somehow finds an audience willing to share in their passion. From nowhere, they reach and involve like-minded music lovers, building enough of a loyal and dedicated following to break into their national music charts off their own back – all without a national TV show launch-pad or a major record company backing them at every turn. 5 Seconds of Summer are such a phenomenon.

In the week after the band's self-titled debut album hit the Number One spot in the US, selling more than a quarter of a million copies, 5SOS's future mentor, musician and record producer John Feldmann stressed in *Billboard* magazine, 'There was no formulaic Simon Cowell-finding-a-bunch-of-handsome-guys. It's just six-foot-three dudes from Australia who loved the same kind of music and put a band together.' It felt more like a mission statement than a retelling of the facts. When Luke, Michael, Calum and Ashton, a group of down-to-earth lads from Sydney, got together to perform their favourite songs, and then decided to share them with the world via videos on YouTube, no one could have predicted that in the space of just over two years they would be releasing chart-topping records around the world and playing sell-out live shows to millions of adoring fans.

The story of 5 Seconds of Summer is not simply the story of a rock band from Australia who conquered the world with a bunch of infectious songs; it's much more than that. It's the story of a mini-revolution. It's the tale of four teenagers who not only understood the power of music and how it can unite a group of people, but who also fully embraced the potential of the internet and social media to engage, and then stay connected to, their ever-expanding 5SOS family. By using the likes of YouTube, Facebook, Twitter, Instagram and every other platform to stay in constant contact with their loyal fans, they have created an army of supporters, willing to follow them wherever their incredible success story takes them. With over six-and-a-half million 'Likes' on the band's official Facebook page, a combined Twitter following in excess of 10 million and close to 100 million views on YouTube for their video at the time of writing, the band has one of the largest active fan bases in the world … ever! Add sold-out concerts across the planet and two globe-trotting tours opening for One Direction, and their amassed worldwide audience would undoubtedly be the envy of the most established of touring bands. What is even more incredible is the fact that most of this was achieved before they had signed a major record deal or released their debut album. When you finally factor in the widespread success of their singles, EPs and albums, it's easy to see that 5 Seconds of Summer, along with the all-important 5SOS family, are more a force a of nature than just a band.

This book explores their origins, their road to success and reveals the fans' role in the group's ongoing quest for global domination. You'd better hold on tight. The rollercoaster ride is set to continue as Luke, Michael, Calum and Ashton scream 'Don't Stop' and ask you to be their 'perfect' companion as they continue taking on the world.

CHAPTER ONE

LUKE HEMMINGS: SHY GUY

'Honestly guys, I'm pretty sure that I'm the same height as the other members in the band.'
LUKE HEMMINGS (@LUKE5SOS), TWITTER

At the point that 5 Seconds of Summer were on the verge of breaking into the American charts for the first time with their *She Looks So Perfect* EP, *Billboard* magazine decided to run a catch-up story entitled '10 Things You Need To Know About 5 Seconds of Summer' for anyone not quite up to speed on the pop sensations newly arrived from Down Under. Predicting the four lads from Australia were poised and ready to dominate the US charts, they singled out the band's lead singer and guitarist for special attention, labelling him 'The Heartthrob'. They went on to describe him: 'He's got the lip ring, the perfectly coiffed blond hair, the disarming smile, the devastating blue eyes,' and boldly stated, 'At this point, his HSP (Harry Styles Potential) is off the charts.' While it's hard to argue with any of this, there's a lot more to Luke Hemmings than his looks. His path to becoming the band's charismatic front man has not been plain sailing, and when you consider he is the youngest of the 5SOS lads, his commitment to the group's future and the sacrifices he has made to ensure its success are all the more extraordinary.

Luke Robert Hemmings was born on 16 July 1996 and was raised, alongside his elder brothers Ben and Jack, by parents Andrew and Liz in Riverstone, a suburb of Sydney, Australia. Luke, like the other future members of his band, Michael Clifford, Calum Hood and Ashton Irwin, was not born into a privileged family, a fact that Ashton, the group's drummer, confirmed to *Billboard*: 'None of us come from a lot of money … we're not from a very nice area.'

As one of the earliest settlements on the outskirts of Sydney, situated approximately 50 km west of the city, Riverstone has become a typically nondescript commuter town, with little in the way of employment opportunities. Most of its 6,000 residents make the daily round-trip to Sydney, taking jobs in one of Australia's busiest and most cosmopolitan cities. Over the years, Riverstone's population has grown as accommodation costs have soared in Sydney's smarter suburbs, and much of the community spirit it once possessed has been eroded by the new arrivals. The town has seen its reputation slide, as certain sections of the town are deemed unsafe at night. Ashton called it 'proper violent' when talking to the *Guardian* some time later, saying the area was virtually 'under curfew' as gangs of teenagers, with nothing to do and energy to burn took to the streets to entertain themselves and ended up drinking, staying out late and generally making trouble.

Although they were not always the closest of friends growing up, all the boys were raised in this environment. It's easy to see how their shared experiences and the hardships that came from living there strengthened their resolve to make a better life for themselves. It's this point Ashton was keen to stress when talking to *Rock Sound* magazine some time later: 'We're not from elaborate mansions in the countryside, we're from suburbs and struggling families.' He went on to explain that their initial interest in music, and subsequent desire to be in a band, was largely fuelled by a need to escape. 'We really tried to build something for ourselves because we didn't want to be where we lived.'

Like many of the early towns in Australia, Riverstone has a number of small churches of varying denominations, set within a small town boundary, and several of the local private schools reflect these religious affiliations. As with the local state-run schools, they provide an all-round education, but with a focus on the values and teachings associated with their particular faith. Luke's parents had forked out to send him to one of these private schools, Norwest Christian College, where he received much of his formal education, and it was here he later met his fellow 5 Seconds of Summer band mates, Michael Clifford and Calum Hood.

Norwest Christian College was founded over thirty years ago, and maintains very high standards in order to ensure all students graduate as well-adjusted and fully rounded individuals. With annual fees of around $7,000, it promises to focus on Christian values, but also strives to give its students a solid academic foundation in life, as well as allowing space for personal development, promoting a sense of individuality and backing every student's basic freedom to express themselves creatively. College Principal Ian Maynard lays out the school objectives on their website: ' … that each child in our care learns to maintain a vibrant inner life full of hope and optimism driven by their own sense of purpose.' The school tries to deliver on three main goals: a strong education, delivered in a nurturing environment and instilling each student with enough self-belief and maturity to make their own important life decisions with confidence and clarity. Maynard goes on to state, 'All three of these elements together enable a child to equip themselves with the skills, knowledge and self-confidence to discover and pursue their purpose with passion and intent.'

It was in this environment that Luke was first encouraged to pursue his love of music and find a way to fully develop his talents for singing and guitar playing, alongside his other more academic studies. Luke's mother, Liz, was for many years a maths teacher, and he inherited her aptitude in the subject, and also showed an early interest in science. But from a very young age there was really only one subject that could capture Luke's full attention: music would quickly become his overriding passion. Singing and learning to play guitar were virtually the only things he wanted to do inside and outside of school, an obsession that would eventually take over much of his free time and ultimately dominate the rest of Luke's teenage years.

Fortunately, there was plenty of support at home and at school, and there would be numerous opportunities to share his talent with his fellow students. The school made sure everyone interested in the performing arts, or with a desire to produce their own music, was given everything they needed to make their dream a reality. With a well-stocked music room and space to rehearse, the school gained quite a reputation as a hotbed of musical talent. It wasn't unusual for the teachers to set up instruments and amplifiers around the campus grounds, encouraging the pupils to perform for each other during break time and giving them valuable experience practising in front of an audience. With its grounds filled with such a vibrant and creative energy, Norwest College became a very positive and inspiring foundation for Luke, his fellow students, and in time for his future band, 5 Seconds of Summer.

As a child, Luke displayed all the qualities his band mates would later cite as his strongest points. Described as 'chirpy', 'fun' and 'always happy', Luke was living a very contented life. He described himself as a 'bit chubby', stating that he was jealous of Calum's skinny physique when he first met him, but looking at his slender, six-foot frame today, it's hard to imagine it was ever a genuine problem. However, it does seem that this tendency to over-indulge may still haunt him a little to this day, the other 5 Seconds boys saying in an online video that he is the one member of the group who can 'eat dinner, then a second dinner, then go to the movies and get a large popcorn and jumbo drink', Michael adding, 'then he might even go get a snack'.

When Luke entered his teenage years, like most boys his age, he began to get much more interested in girls. He says he has never been attracted to any particular physical types, and told *Top of the Pops* magazine, 'I'm just looking for someone who likes me and is comfortable in their own skin.' It suggests that his more serious outlook on life means he is seeking something long-term, rather than simply a fling. Unfortunately for Luke, he could at times be a little awkward, and this became even more exaggerated around girls, meaning he would often feel out of his depth on those uncomfortable first dates. He recalled one typical failure to impress a girl: 'I'm clumsy when I get nervous and spilled soy sauce all over myself at a sushi restaurant.' But one girl in particular was about to catch his eye, and soon she would become a constant companion and an endless source of inspiration.

Aleisha McDonald was also a student at Norwest with a talent for singing and playing guitar, and it wasn't long before the pair began hanging out together and, eventually, they started dating. Very quickly, Aleisha became more than just Luke's girlfriend; she also became his singing partner and they would perform together around the school campus and for friends and family, and even uploaded a couple of videos to YouTube. The standouts among these are the pair's cover of Maroon 5's 'She Will Be Loved', and a live performance of A Day To Remember's 'If It Means a Lot to You', filmed in the Norwest College grounds. Their relationship continued through 2012, but when Luke's commitment to 5 Seconds of Summer meant he was spending more and more time away from home touring, and later took an extended trip to London, it became unmanageable, and the couple decided it was best to split up.

Encouraged by Luke's early success, Aleisha began to host her own video channel, and collaborated with other musicians, including her younger brother, Shannon. Citing Alicia Keys, Beyoncé, James Vincent McMorrow and English indie-folk band, Daughter, among her main influences and inspirations, it's clear she wants to differentiate herself from Luke and the rest of the 5SOS lads in terms of the music she makes. Having completed her high school certificate, she continues to pursue music as a career, uploading covers to her channel, and recently announced she'd had the opportunity to record some of her original songs in a proper studio, taking to Twitter to say, 'I've been writing songs non-stop for so long now. I hope I can show them to you some time soon.'

Her connection to Luke and her status as his ex-girlfriend has meant Aleisha has had to face more than her fair share of negative comments, suffering some unnecessary abuse from certain sections of 5SOS's fan base. She has tried to maintain a close relationship with Luke, and often sends him tweets. When asked what Luke was really like on Ask.fm, she said, 'Luke is absolutely the most perfect and amazing person I've ever met! He is such a nice boy and a good friend. Still my best friend.' In recent times, she has tried to distance herself from being known simply as 'Luke's ex' – in July 2014 she was forced to shut down her personal Twitter account, stating she needed to step away from the site in order to concentrate on her school qualifications, but also admitted it was due to her feed being bombarded continually by online trolls and to combat a number of fake accounts pretending to be her by using her name.

Luke's friendship with Aleisha is probably the most publicized of the 5 Seconds boys' early relationships, and it's testament to Luke's affection for Aleisha that he has remained tight-lipped about their time together. More recently, he has spoken openly about the frustrations he and the other boys sometimes feel trying to build meaningful relationships during the intense, early stages of their career, stating it is virtually impossible to even consider starting anything serious. Similarly, Ashton told radio station KIIS 1065, 'We don't have girlfriends. It's not a rule, it's just a thing … We're not in the same place for more than twenty-four hours usually, so it's just hard to commit to anything.' Instead, Luke admits he seeks solace in the bonds he's made with his fellow band members, telling Fuse online, 'As a band we are stronger and a proper little family.'

Spending time away from his real family and making new friends was never something Luke was particularly good at as a child. As the youngest member of the band, and with a particularly close-knit family, it has probably been hardest for him to deal with the long trips away from home. The band's stay in London in September 2012 was the first time he'd left Australia, and during their second London visit later that year, Luke was the only one of the four who flew home to Sydney to be with his family during the Christmas break. It is this strong connection with family that has kept Luke firmly grounded, so far avoiding any 'superstar tantrums' or 'diva behaviour'. Liz, his mother, is always quick to welcome Luke back from his international travels, but is equally hasty to bring him back down to earth. In the past, she has taken to Twitter to say, 'It's good to have Luke home but boy he is messy,' while on another occasion she proclaimed, 'Packages delivered to airport. Look out Oz, 5SOS is on its way. Luke ya didn't make ur bed when ya left …'

Alongside missing his family, Luke also had the added

complication of not being able to finish his high school education before the band set off on their endless voyages. When important exams loomed, his mother had tried to help Luke with his work. Liz headed out on tour with the band, aiding her son and the other boys with their studies, but in the end it all proved too complicated. As the group's touring schedule and workload increased dramatically, Luke had to abandon all hope of achieving anything close to the exam results he knew he was capable of. Although it's unlikely he will be too concerned about his lack of academic qualifications now a bright future with 5 Seconds of Summer seems assured, as a conscientious individual it can't have been easy for him to give up on his formal education. Yet, while there is no doubt Luke's schooling shaped him in many ways, it is his mother, and his home life, that has had just as much of an impact on his character.

It is often pointed out by the other members of the band that Luke, while a happy individual, is also the most serious of the boys in 5SOS, and has repeatedly shown in interviews that he is more of a thinker than a talker. By far the quietest, he is also the most level-headed member of the group. Calum said in one of their online videos, '[Luke always] chooses the sensible thing to do,' while Ashton, commenting on how the two-year age gap between them means he has taken a 'brotherly' role in Luke's life, said, 'I feel I've seen him grow up into a mini-man.' This maturity and balance may stem from the fact that his home life has proved to be the most stable of all the boys' – his parents' marriage has remained intact and he has the strong influence of male role models in the shape of his father and two older brothers.

With a house full of teenage boys, the Hemmings family home was always a lively place to be. Luke was an active child, enjoying playing soccer with his siblings, as well as being a keen skateboarder – perhaps this is where he gets his 'amazing legs', Luke's best feature, according to Michael. All members of the Hemmings family enjoyed winter sports, and Luke showed particular skills at snowboarding. His love of music, however, seems to have little to do with his upbringing, as his parents and brothers have never shown much interest in the subject. In fact, when asked where he got his musical talent from, his mother joked with Australia's *60 Minutes*, 'Not from me. No one likes to hear me sing.' Wherever it came from, it started early, took hold very quickly and has stayed with him his whole life.

Luke states Good Charlotte were his favourite band growing up – 2003's *The Young and the Hopeless* was the first album he ever bought and they were also the first band he saw in concert. His taste in music is probably broader than any other member of 5 Seconds of Summer, judging from the wide variety of artists he chose to cover in his first batch of YouTube videos. From Bruno Mars and Ed Sheeran to Mayday Parade and A Day To Remember, and the subsequent early 5SOS covers, including Blink-182, All Time Low and the likes of Busted, Adele and One Direction, it's hard to identify which genre is his preference. It would seem the only thing that they have in common is the quality of the songs themselves, suggesting Luke showed an early appreciation of strong melodies and well-constructed lyrics, something that would later prove invaluable when writing his own songs.

Music is clearly a very personal and private enjoyment for Luke. It's not hard to pick up on his lack of confidence in the earliest YouTube videos, as he avoids looking directly at the camera and gives each song minimal introduction. But his singing and playing abilities strengthened, and his self-belief was bolstered by positive online feedback and then the support of Aleisha. It's easy to see that by the time he started spending more time with Michael, and eventually Calum, he was more than ready to take his music to the next level and start his own band. What is surprising is Calum's revelation that the three boys' meeting was hardly love at first sight. He stated in one of their online videos, 'Michael didn't like Luke at first, and I was best friends with Michael at the time, so I actually didn't like him.' He then confessed, 'But in the back of my mind, I was like, "He seems like a really cool guy."' Luke was quick to point out that the feeling was most definitely mutual, adding, 'We actually hated each other for a solid year of my life.' Michael confirmed that those feelings of distrust ran deep: 'In Year 9, we hated each other, he wanted to kill me and I wanted to kill him, and then in Year 10 we became best friends.'

Before hooking up with his future 5SOS 'brothers', Luke was always a little shy around new people, something that could often make him uptight and clumsy, and he would end up avoiding the popular children in school. He was much more of a loner, content to spend hours practising his guitar playing, singing and learning new songs. In order to fit in at school, Luke spent time with groups of people he didn't really know, or have much in common with, leading to some incidents of teasing and bullying. One such incident saw Luke being defended by his future band mate, Ashton Irwin, although at that point they didn't know each other very well. He told Vevo, 'It's not that dramatic … I was with some people that I didn't really like too much and Ashton was along with them … I'd just got a haircut and [the others] were teasing me about it. Ashton was like, "Leave the boy alone."'

Ashton recalled his first proper meeting with Luke, which took place at a local cinema, when Luke was being teased yet again by so-called friends. This time they were picking on him because of the glasses he was wearing, and Ashton simply introduced himself to Luke, and said, 'Hi, I'm Ashton,' before telling him he thought his glasses were actually 'kinda cool'.

Although contact had been made, it would be some time later before Luke and Ashton would become true friends. While returning to their separate social circles, both boys were actually much happier in their own company, playing or listening to music, escaping to their own worlds. It was this subtle, nagging feeling of being outcasts – one eventually echoed by his fellow Norwest students, Michael Clifford and Calum Hood – that would become the glue that bound the band of (slightly dysfunctional) brothers and laid the foundations for their first tentative steps towards forming their own group.

CHAPTER TWO

MICHAEL CLIFFORD: WALK ON THE WILD SIDE

'No TV, check. No wi-fi, check. No signal, check. Only enough hot water for one shower, check. Not near civilization, check. #5soshouse LOL.'
MICHAEL CLIFFORD (@MICHAEL5SOS), TWITTER

In an online video the boys uploaded, introducing their new fans to the individual members of the group, Michael was described by the others as 'weird', 'nerdy', 'sloppy', 'sassy' and, rather damningly, only 'slightly funny'. When later asked by *Seventeen* magazine to describe his fellow band mate, Calum Hood branded 5 Seconds of Summer's lead guitarist as 'the wild one'. While he has some way to go before challenging Ozzy Osbourne as the crazy man of rock, Michael Clifford certainly has an adventurous side. Perhaps the clearest indication of his rebellious streak, and the feature that sets him apart from the rest of 5SOS, is his hair – permanently awry, with its 'punk' spikes and ever-changing rainbow of colours – over the last few years alone it has been faded pink, luminous pink, green, blue, purple and, very occasionally, his natural dark blond. It was the first thing the rest of the boys remember about meeting Michael, with Calum going as far as to call it 'fringe-tastic'.

But far from being just a walking hairstyle, Michael is keen to show he has true punk credentials. He has a very bad habit of wearing (accidentally) ripped jeans – sometimes barely covering his modesty and usually for a few more consecutive days than hygienically acceptable – and his wardrobe is bursting with sleeveless plaid shirts, undoubtedly making him the most 'rock 'n' roll' member of the group. Unfortunately, this status may be in jeopardy after admitting to *Coup De Main* magazine that he has 'My Little Pony underwear'. When not sporting garments featuring small horses, Michael can invariably be seen wearing a wide range of vintage rock band T-shirts, from Iron Maiden, Def Leppard and Metallica to The Rolling Stones, Neil Young and The B-52s. There is no doubting where his musical allegiances lie, and Michael has one foot (or should that be one ear?) firmly in the past. It's fair to say that the band's gigs at the legendary rock venue The Forum in Los Angeles was a high point of his particular 5 Seconds of Summer journey so far.

With the reputation of being by far the untidiest member of the group, his band mates have often questioned Michael's cleanliness, complaining in a Vevo interview that his room smelled of poppadoms, despite Michael insisting he hadn't eaten one for years. He has also gained a reputation for spending too much time in bed or asleep when the boys are on a day off. It seems this is a habit he picked up during his early teens, when he would spend weeks on end, alone, in his bedroom, plugged into his beloved game console. In one of their online videos, Ashton describes Michael as 'secluded' during the period before he joined the band, while Calum tells it more frankly, saying Michael had been effectivelly 'cooped away in his room for about five years'. Perhaps due to all the compulsive gaming, Michael labels himself as being 'slightly OCD', and despite the other boys' doubts, he says he washes his hands 'up to twenty times a day'.

Arguably because of his OCD tendencies, he gets bored and distracted very quickly. This in turn means he likes to keep things unpredictable when it comes to interviews, with answers often veering off into fantasy. He's generally known for not taking anything very seriously, and in an early Vevo introductory video interview, when all the other boys explained that they came from Sydney, Australia, Michael insisted he was in fact from 'Middle-earth, in Narnia'. He is always the first to break away from whatever he is supposed to be doing, ignoring the job at hand and forcing the others into mischief or pranks, best exemplified by the chaos that invariably ensues during many of their online videos. As the most carefree member of 5 Seconds of Summer, Michael helps keep the rest of the boys on their toes, but he is also the one who brings the most energy to their performances and injects an element of humour into much of their music.

Born on 20 November 1995, Michael Gordon Clifford grew up as an only child, raised by his mother, Karen, in the same Riverstone neighbourhood as his future 5 Seconds of Summer band mates, Luke Hemmings and Calum Hood. He also attended Norwest Christian College, sharing the other boys' status as outsiders at the school, although his lack of social standing seems to have more to do with his love of gaming, spending much of his free time alone at his computer, than any particular issue with socializing or making friends. Most importantly, he also has the same love of listening to and playing music, which would eventually bring the three core members of the group together.

Michael's taste in music is probably the most punk of any member of the band, citing the likes of All Time Low, and particularly Sum 41, as his favourite bands. In an interview with *Alternative Press*, he said of the band's hit song, 'In Too Deep', 'If I had to show someone what pop-punk was, it would be this song … I think it's the perfect mix of what should be on the radio.' While Michael certainly brings the heaviest and most guitar-driven influences to the table, it's not to say he doesn't love his fair share of 'guilty pleasure' music, admitting he has a weakness for rapper T-Pain and tweeting endlessly about his fascination with Nickelback and his ability to sing along to every track on their *All the Right Reasons* album.

At school, he more or less preferred to keep himself to himself, and at home he would be locked away with his game console or be trying to pick up tips on how to play his guitar. All these extra-curricular activities meant Michael didn't have much time left over for studying, and his grades suffered as a result. It was clear to him that it had to be music or bust, something he confirmed in an interview with Singapore Radio, when he confessed that if he wasn't in a band he would struggle to imagine what else he would be doing: 'The other boys would probably have jobs and stuff, but I, 100 per cent, would be doing nothing.'

His love of guitars came very young. He told the Gibson website that his first real guitar was an Epiphone Les Paul, a budget version of one of Gibson's most famous guitars, and all these years later he still plays a Gibson Joan Jett Signature Melody Maker. On one of 5 Seconds of Summer's earliest trips to the UK, Michael was lucky enough to be invited to the esteemed Gibson guitar showroom in London. Thrilled to visit this guitar heaven, it only fuelled his obsession even more, as he explained: 'It was insane, I just walked into this room full of guitars … They let me borrow one and [I] have been playing them ever since. Thank you, Gibson!'

As time passed, it was his love of playing guitar, and his

appreciation of others with similar talents, that saw him slowly gravitate towards Luke at Norwest. While Michael has said he knew who Luke was for a long time before they finally spoke, saying he was unsure whether the pair would get along, and even going as far as saying they 'hated each other', his distrust slowly started to subside. The more he saw of Luke's talent, the more he was convinced he had found a musical soulmate. Soon he was spending every spare moment he had 'banding' – the made-up word the boys used for their early practice sessions and rehearsals.

Michael was probably the most confident of the boys in his own musical abilities, and he acquired an early, unwavering faith in the band's likelihood to succeed, even when those around them doubted their dream. Adam Day, their Norwest College music tutor, told the *Sydney Morning Herald*, 'Michael always said to me, "I'm going to be a superstar one day" … That was his dream from Year 9 on. I remember him coming off stage from a performance one evening and he said, "Yeah, that's what I'm going to do. I'm going to be famous one day. Watch out."'

While his school results didn't quite match the boast – Michael admitted to the *Daily Mail*, 'I got a D in music' – his old music teacher was willing to give Michael credit where it was due. He said to the *Australian*, 'Michael used to say to me that he was going to be a rock star one day, which I used to brush off lightly.' He finished, 'He's one of those guys who proved me wrong.'

Despite his tendency to hide himself away, Michael did find time to socialize a little, and he counted future band mate, Calum Hood, as one of his closest friends. Calum would later say on one of the band's online videos, 'He's always there to cheer you up when you're down. He's just a great friend overall, really.'

And as far as girls are concerned, Michael dated a few through high school, but nothing developed into anything particularly serious, and once the band started to take up more of his time, his focus shifted almost exclusively to music. When asked what his ideal girl would be like, Michael told Vevo that he liked 'girls who I can do nothing with and still have a good time'. He also revealed to *Top of the Pops* magazine, 'My dream girl would be funny, weird and caring. I don't know if I've met her yet, but then maybe I have and just haven't known it.' Confessing he 'sent flowers to a girl who had a boyfriend', but that he 'honestly didn't know', and that he once serenaded a girl with a version of Justin Bieber's 'One Less Lonely Girl', it might just explain why he's been single most of the time!

Michael was, however, briefly linked to Hollywood actress Abigail Breslin in August 2013. The *Daily Mail* ran a story about the teen star of *Little Miss Sunshine* and *Ender's Game* leaving a Los Angeles restaurant after presenting at the Teen Choice Awards, stating she had 'ditched her glam dress in favour of something a little more alternative as she headed out with her male pal'. As this was just after the US leg of the

One Direction tour had ended and 5 Seconds of Summer had not yet gained the global recognition they now have, it's understandable Michael managed to slip under the radar and end up referred to as merely an unknown 'male companion'. Whether or not the date turned into anything more serious is still a well-kept secret, but Abigail did post the following intriguing message on her Twitter account later that night, saying, 'Well ... Today has certainly been interesting.'

Michael's list of celebrity crushes may or may not include Abigail, but he did have an online flirtation with Camila Cabello, a member of US girl group Fifth Harmony, and told the Hollywood Life website, during a game of 'snog, marry or avoid', that he would definitely want to marry Miley Cyrus, before quickly joking, 'I take it back. Miley's not ready for marriage.'

In truth, like the other members of the band, Michael has very little time for anything except eating and sleeping outside of their busy work schedule, but when the moment allows, he will always make time for his game console and his computer. His obsession with Twitter is legendary – there's a reason why a huge proportion of his time on the road is spent complaining about the lack of Wi-Fi in hotel rooms – but it's not something he shares with his mother, Karen. When asked by *60 Minutes* if she kept in touch with her son's antics via the social networking site, she said, 'I keep away from anything with a 'Tw' – Twitter, Twerking and *Twilight* movies.'

Of all the boys, Michael seems to have the greatest desire

to see the band move towards a more 'serious' rock sound as their careers progress. This obviously stems from his own personal tastes, but it is also reflected in the creative input he's already had in the songs the boys have recorded over the last couple of years. Michael has co-written seven tracks featured across the different standard versions of their debut album, and his influence has clearly signalled a move away from the softer, more poppy sound of their very first songs to the much darker and more guitar-driven tones of 'Good Girls', '18' and 'End Up Here'.

However strong his influence is on the band's overall feel, Michael is the first to admit that it is the chemistry between all four boys that makes the group so special. In early 2011, as his friendship with Luke had started to evolve and their commitment to keep practising was resulting in long jamming sessions at school and at each other's home, things were beginning to gel. Michael told the US TV show *Extra*, 'I think when we started, we were just doing it for fun and, I mean, then eventually we got serious about it and we realized, wow, this could be something. And we just worked our butts off.'

Part of that process was the addition of an extra member of the 'banding' club – the boys were about to become a three-piece, and Michael's friend Calum Hood would be the next important piece of the puzzle to fall into place.

CHAPTER THREE

CALUM HOOD: TAKE IT EASY

'Planning on living forever.'
CALUM HOOD (@CALUM5SOS), TWITTER

'I'm just the chill dude' is how Calum Hood described himself in an interview with *Seventeen* magazine, and while this is undoubtedly the impression many get of 5 Seconds of Summer's bass player, a laid-back approach to life is only one aspect of this go-getter's character.

In their online video introductions, Luke reinforces the idea Calum is easygoing, stating, 'He is always relaxed in the most stressful situations,' while Ashton praises the fact Calum is 'always up for some adventure'. Michael, on the other hand, jokingly insists Calum is 'actually the weirdest person in the band but refuses to admit it'. All the boys comment on Calum's physical appearance, calling him 'streamline', 'hairless', 'a cuddly little bear' and perhaps somewhat disturbingly, 'like a naked mole-rat'.

Calum's earliest involvement with the band proved to be vitally important. As the third member of the group to join in on the Norwest jamming sessions, alongside the newly bonded Luke and Michael, Calum provided the all-important impetus that turned their casual get-togethers from shambolic 'banding' into something much more organized. Soon they were setting up structured group guitar lessons and attending proper rehearsals. By getting the boys to focus on their playing, sharing his musical influences and helping them take their first steps towards writing their own songs, Calum had laid the first real foundations for turning them from three lads playing guitars in a garage into the earliest version of the 5 Seconds of Summer we know today.

Calum Thomas Hood was born on 25 January 1996 in Sydney, New South Wales. The Hood household consisted of his mother, Joy, his father, David and elder sister, Mali-Koa, and Calum's arrival completed their small family unit. Calum has the most exotic ancestry of the band, often mistakenly thought to be Asian: his mother was born in Auckland, New Zealand, while his father's family originated on the other side of the world in Scotland.

Indeed, there was a strong British cultural influence on Calum's upbringing, and this can best be seen in his love of soccer and the fact that he still actively follows and supports Liverpool FC to this day. In fact, his interest in soccer became a very important part of his childhood, as he showed an early aptitude for the game and pursued it as a hobby for many years. As his skills increased, he was chosen as part of a team sent to Brazil to represent Australia, but eventually had to give it up when his music started to take up more and more of his free time. When 5 Seconds started to make a name for themselves, Calum told his local newspaper, the *Rouse Hill Times*, 'Every now and then I put the boots back on, but for now it's one hundred per cent focusing on the music.' While the thought of playing professionally is a dim and distant memory, Calum insists he still likes to have an occasional kickabout and always cheers on his beloved Liverpool.

Back in high school, having made his decision that music would be his main focus going forward, Calum broke the news to the rest of the Hood family: he wanted to be in a rock band. While obviously a little surprised at first, his mother, Joy, took the news in her stride, later telling *60 Minutes*, 'We kind of thought, "Gosh, I hope he's good at it."'

In fact, the Hood household already had a decent amount of musical pedigree: Calum's sister, Mali-Koa, is also a talented singer-songwriter and took part in Australia's first series of *The Voice* in 2012. Although she made it through the Blind Auditions – coincidentally picked to join the team fronted by future 5SOS collaborator, Good Charlotte's Joel Madden – Mali didn't make it past the Battle Rounds and was eliminated in the show's eighth episode. Mali has continued her singing career, enjoying a strong following in her hometown, and the celebrity status she gained from her appearance on *The Voice* (as well as having a brother in one of the hottest bands in the world) led to her being asked to be a head judge for local singing contest *The Hills Are Alive*. Taking a break from 5 Seconds of Summer's mini Australian tour, Calum even joined his sister on stage for a couple of duets during the show's finale in August 2012, performing covers of Chris Brown's 'Forever' and Katy Perry's 'Teenage Dream'.

Before joining the band, it was with his sister and the rest of his family that Calum felt most relaxed and self-assured. Like all the boys, Calum sometimes struggles being away from home and on the road for long periods of time. He told Sydney's *Daily Telegraph*, 'I always miss my family and friends when I'm on tour, it's just natural.' He also admitted he finds comfort in knowing he's doing it for the right reasons, saying, 'When you're playing to 20,000 people each night, doing what you love, it makes it one hundred times easier.'

Like his future band mate, Luke, he was slightly shy around new people when he was growing up and struggled with his confidence when socializing. It appeared he wasn't entirely sure of himself when it came to dating, either, revealing to *Top of the Pops* magazine, 'I went on a date, but realized I didn't like the girl half way through. That was awkward.' He went on to relate how he is much more certain about his ideal type of girl nowadays, though: 'I like a girl who's quirky, funny and slightly weird … We're weird guys so it needs to be balanced out.'

Describing himself as 'the opposite of a jock' in *Girlfriend* magazine, it seems that Calum's love of soccer may have been his only real concession to becoming a 'team player' at Norwest. Despite the college actively promoting the game as part of their sports programme, soccer has struggled to shake off its 'migrant' roots and become a universally accepted mainstream sport in Australia, and Calum's association with the game may actually have been something that set him apart from the other boys his age, most of whom were more likely to be into surfing, swimming, rugby or basketball. With a passion for music and his status as something of an outsider at Norwest, it wasn't long before he began hanging out with his fellow students, Luke and Michael. Although Michael and Calum were already fairly close at this point, in one of the band's online videos Luke insists, 'I thought I wasn't cool enough to be friends with Calum.'

Calum, it seems, was never officially asked to join Luke and Michael's exclusive 'banding' club, but could soon be found happily singing and playing alongside them. By the spring of 2011, these three very different personalities had found a common goal, Calum admitting to the *Daily Telegraph*, 'When we joined the band we were definitely outcasts – we weren't bullied, but we were outcasts … Being in the band just cemented everything.'

Calum's taste in music is nothing if not diverse. Among the 5SOS lads, he certainly has the most eclectic mix of artists on his iPod, and while he stated in *Girlfriend* that the first song he ever bought was the band's favourite, 'I Miss You' by Blink-182, he also mentioned his love of Chris Brown, Nicki Minaj and American rock band, Boys Like Girls. It was these diverse tastes and an openness to different influences that Calum brought to the band, giving them a unique starting point for their own music.

His ability to write original songs, and his support for the others to do the same, would have an important impact on the band's future output. Calum wrote 'Gotta Get Out', the first original 5 Seconds of Summer song they shared via YouTube and one of the first to get an official release as part of the *Somewhere New* EP. Inspired by their early attempts, and convinced that writing their own songs was the only way forward for the band, Calum's first efforts helped boost the other boys' self-confidence, gave them some clarity about the direction the band should take and encouraged them to fully develop their own individual songwriting abilities. It was this injection of self-belief that would lead the boys to retain a large degree of creative control over everything they would go on to record and release.

Calum is the most prolific songwriter in the group, and he told *Sunday Morning Herald*: 'I spend a lot of time on it. Some days it doesn't come and I'm angry for the whole night.' Writer's block doesn't seem to have been too much of a problem, however, as his contributions to the band's debut album equal Michael's, boasting seven songs, and many others that feature as bonus tracks on EPs or are due to be released.

He shares the same strong work ethic and ambition that drives all four of the band members, as he said to *USA Today*: 'The boys and I have high expectations of what we want to achieve.' But perhaps Calum's more laid-back outlook on life makes him uniquely placed to ensure they all learn to cope with the demands and stresses coming their way on a daily basis. He continued, 'You always feel a bit of pressure ... but we're really just having fun at the moment and taking it day by day.'

In the spring of that year, they began posting videos on YouTube as a three-piece, and on one occasion at least, while Luke was away on holiday, Michael and Calum even made a video as a duo. The pair uploaded themselves joking around and thanking fans for their feedback. Although it acted as little more than a 'we-haven't-really-got-anything-to-say' stop-gap, it highlights the growing camaraderie between the two friends, the crazy humour that would soon become so closely associated with much of the band's output and, perhaps most importantly, it shows the boys' determination to stay in touch with their fans, keeping them involved and up to date with everything 5SOS.

What is apparent from all of these early videos is the increasing chemistry between the three, and while some of the performances are better than others, there's no denying the early signs of potential.

CHAPTER FOUR

'LET'S START A BAND'

'I don't think we try to fool anyone. We're not really that cool. As a band sometimes we might look a little bit cool, but we're just dorky dudes.'
LUKE HEMMINGS, *ROCK SOUND* MAGAZINE

At the beginning of 2011, Luke had summoned up the courage to start posting videos of himself singing and playing guitar on his YouTube channel, Hemmo1996. By the beginning of February, at just fourteen years old, Luke uploaded a cover of Mike Posner's 'Please Don't Go'. In its original form, it is more of an R&B club track, but Luke stripped the song down to expose its simple, heartfelt lyrics and it proved to be a perfect showcase for his soulful vocal style and growing skills on acoustic guitar. It's worth noting that the first person to leave a comment under the video is

Aleisha McDonald, who posted, 'So proud of you youngin.'

Over the next few months, Luke posted several more videos of himself singing and playing. While he was already an accomplished vocalist and was increasingly confident in his abilities with the guitar, he was clearly still self-conscious in front of the camera and the introductions were brief or, in most cases, non-existent. Covers of tracks by artists as diverse as CeeLo Green and lesser-known American and Australian singer-songwriters, Ron Pope and Pete Murray, as well as several rock songs, suggested Luke was still casting his net far and wide for inspiration, and was collecting as many ideas as possible for the direction his own music might take. The focus he needed was about to be supplied by two of his fellow students at Norwest.

Luke and Michael's paths had crossed at school on many occasions over the years, yet they had never really become friends. They were aware of each other but had maintained different social circles, both in and out of school hours. As Michael began to see more of Luke's performances and witnessed a few of his shows in the school grounds, he realized they shared more than just an interest in playing guitar; they also had similar tastes in music. The pair drifted towards each other, and very quickly they were swapping guitar-playing tips and discussing their favourite artists until the idea of starting a band themselves began to surface. Although not officially a part of the group at this point, Calum described the moment that sparked the creation of the band to the Punktastic website: 'Michael was like, "Hey, man, do you wanna start a band?" and Luke was like, "OK."' And, that easily, the pieces fell into place – 'banding' had become 'band'. Soon Norwest College's music room became a regular hangout for Luke and Michael as they started jamming together, learning new songs and generally exploring their shared passion for music. Before long they were joined more frequently by Calum, who said, 'I just kind of wedged myself in there somehow,' and it was here the first seeds of 5 Seconds of Summer's emerging sound and fast-developing chemistry were sown.

The boys' music tastes were broadly similar. They all shared a love of 1990s American pop-punk and rock acts such as Blink-182, Fall Out Boy and Green Day, so it was obvious any group they might dream of forming would be inspired by these bands' sounds. Luke later explained their collective thinking: 'We like making music that we love, to be our own favourite band.' Ashton explained this idea: 'I used to be weird about saying that, but one of my favourite bands are Paramore and they say that they're their own favourite band. They make their music how they like it.' It became clear very early on that while 5 Seconds of Summer's sound might end up being a mix of very different styles, incorporating not only the rock elements of their best-loved bands, but also some of their less conventional preferences, they were going to make their music their own way.

Indeed, this range of styles could first be seen in Luke's

earliest videos, in part because his interests lay not only in emulating the energy and power of his favourite rock songs, but also in capturing what made a record sound great on the radio. He wanted to crystallize the element that sent certain artists' songs into the mainstream music charts, thus he was as likely to study and perform a track by Maroon 5 or Adele as he was his beloved Good Charlotte. Altogether, it would form quite a powerful mix of influences and push the sound they were creating into an area far more commercial and accessible than their lists of favourite acts might suggest.

No doubt the Norwest College music room became a fun and creative environment for the boys. Initially no one at school paid them much attention, and any thoughts that being in a band would improve their social status or increase their popularity with the girls at school were quickly squashed, as Luke explained to the *Sydney Morning Herald*: 'If you weren't a footballer then you weren't attractive.' If they were being ignored by their fellow students, thankfully they received plenty of support from the Norwest staff. One of the college's music teachers, Adam Day, recalled, 'I started teaching them music in Year 7, and they excelled in all the practical activities of [the subject].' He acknowledged their only problem was that '[They] were very quiet and shy and reserved ... [but] were very much closet musos.' He was quick to spot the boys' early potential and offered vital encouragement whenever he could. 'I wrote on their reports back then that it would be good to seek performance opportunities to develop their confidence.'

It was a great piece of advice, and one that the boys eventually took on board. At this point they had only just started performing in front of their friends and family, but as they became ever more confident, they began to realize Mr Day was right – they needed to allow everyone else to see what they could do. It's hard to imagine now, but soon the band were asking for gigs on their official Facebook page, letting it be known they were available to play at birthday parties, school dances and private events in the Sydney area. They even encouraged fans to send them requests via their personal Facebook inboxes. The site would surely crash very quickly if they did the same today!

The boys were still having fun, and none of them were taking the idea of being in a real band too seriously. But serious or not, they realized they should start thinking about a name for their band if they were going to start advertising their services for shows. It was Michael who eventually came up with the name 5 Seconds of Summer while daydreaming in maths class one day in April. He wanted something fans could add their own name to – like 5 Seconds of Michael or 5 Seconds of Luke, and he told 96.5 TIC FM in Connecticut, 'I sent [the other guys in the band] a message and said, "Hey, guys, I'm naming the band 5 Seconds of Summer," and they were like, "Okay, we're cool with that."' Although they might have accepted the name with a shrug, secretly, as Michael told the OCC website, they 'hated it'. It now seems clear no one really imagined the name would be around for long; they were just a college band after all, goofing around and enjoying themselves. Luke reasoned, 'When you're in a band in school, you just pick your name because you're not expecting it to last very long.' Whether or not Luke was thinking about the long term, his YouTube channel eventually changed from Hemmo1996 to 5 Seconds of Summer, and even if there was a moment of doubt – such as when the band's Facebook page suggested on 11 April 2011 that 'Bromance' was perhaps a better name for a band – Michael's original idea seemed to stick.

As things progressed, the other two boys started joining Luke on more of the YouTube videos, and a steady stream of new covers were uploaded over the course of 2011. A cover of Blink-182's rock ballad, 'I Miss You', and A Day To Remember's 'If It Means a Lot to You', perhaps show some of the influence Michael and Calum were having on the group's musical direction, but it would be their cover of Chris Brown's collaboration with Justin Bieber, 'Next to You', which, at that point, gave the boys their most-watched video. Their performances were often rough and ready, with the boys forgetting words, playing wrong notes and generally fooling around, but, nevertheless, they were making headway. Michael and Calum continued to post content while Luke was away on holiday, although it was more of a reminder to their fans that they hadn't forgotten them and new videos would be coming soon.

Flying under the radar of their Norwest classmates, the

5SOS boys realized this online audience – the people who had tuned in regularly to catch their latest upload – was worth nurturing for the future. They kept them engaged, constantly asking for feedback for their most recent efforts and prompting them to make requests for the songs they wanted to hear the group perform. 5 Seconds had launched their official Facebook page in early spring and by the end of May they had already passed 3,000 'Likes'. The band then started interacting directly with their fans, using the Ustream video streaming service to host online chats and keep everyone up to date with the latest developments, events and videos. They also wanted to make sure that every one of this first wave of fans was aware of their own special part in the band's growing popularity. By the middle of June, 5 Seconds had 8,000 'Likes' on Facebook and had started an official 5 Seconds of Summer Twitter account. Word was spreading online, and the 5SOS family was growing rapidly.

All of this was a welcome release from their regular lessons, and the boys quickly formed a very strong bond of friendship, built around the chemistry they shared when they picked up their instruments. And it wasn't long before the response from their active social networking made them realize they might be on to something after all, leading them to begin preparing more seriously for public appearances together. Soon they would be performing on a grander scale, and that required a much more professional approach.

By September, they had posted details of an event at a local

Sydney cinema, 'An Afternoon at the Cinema – Unplugged', which would see the band playing their first free public concert alongside another young pop-punk band, Some Time Soon. As the promoters put it, they were 'two Australian up-and-comers', and listed 5SOS's impressive social media stats: 100,000 hits on YouTube, 14,000 subscribers to their channel and almost 20,000 fans on Facebook. They stated, 'Not bad for three young dudes from Sydney', before urging everyone to come along and 'see what all the fuss is about'. And come they did, even if it wasn't quite in the vast numbers they would in time come to expect.

Some Time Soon were a significantly more established band, with a solid following in their native Adelaide. They had already released their debut EP, made a music video and had toured extensively across Australia. It is probable that, despite not having the home-crowd advantage, they were the bigger band on the bill. Although they had a comparative lack of experience, the 5SOS lads played a rapturously received acoustic set, including some of the covers they had already performed on YouTube, and counted the show as a major step forward in helping them build confidence as performers. It also gave them valuable experience in front of an audience who may not necessarily have come to see only them perform. It immediately spurred the boys on to move to the next level – they wanted to play their own gig, in a proper rock venue, and show everyone exactly what they could do.

Flushed with the success of the cinema event, that same month they were offered a gig at one of Sydney's coolest rock venues, the Annandale Hotel, in two and a half months' time. The manager of the venue tracked the boys down on Facebook, messaged them and asked if they wanted to play a proper gig, and the deal was quickly struck. The Annandale's small music room was a 'no frills' space, but it had gained notoriety over the years and had grown from a simple late-night spot to become one of the most iconic rock venues in Australia, playing host to hundreds of home-grown and international rock acts.

While performing at the Annandale would undoubtedly bring the boys some rock 'n' roll credibility, it wasn't an obvious match for a group of teenagers still wet behind the ears and fresh from posting Justin Bieber songs on YouTube. The lads' determination to avoid the fate of other boy bands – lip-synching to backing tracks in nightclubs or playing free gigs in local malls – and desire to be seen as a proper group that played real instruments meant they would be forced to compete with much more experienced acts, and face the crowds that followed them. Reflecting on the gig later, Ashton explained to *Rock Sound*, 'Sydney underground bands and bands in general are very heavy … It's very hardcore, and we wanted to be a rock band like Green Day. We didn't really fit.' He continued, 'The different thing with us was that girls would come to see us. Their crowds would just be sweaty dudes and they hated us.' He expanded on this in an interview with the *Sydney Morning Herald*: 'We used to have to go and play shows with metal bands at the Annandale ... they told us we were bad every single day.' It was also a test of endurance for the boys' small, but loyal, female fan base. Ashton recalled, 'We had barely any fans but they would be so dedicated ... coming to the Annandale Hotel when you are barely sixteen and a girl is not ideal.'

If it seemed like a step too far for the fans, what about for the boys themselves? They began to question whether, by December, they'd really be ready to showcase their material at such a venue. Performing as an acoustic three-piece – with three voices and three guitars – was one thing, but to become a proper, self-contained band and progress their sound to the required level, 5 Seconds of Summer would need to create their own rhythm section – bass guitar and drums – and that would mean some major changes to the structure of the group.

Solving the bass problem was easy enough, as the self-confessed 'worst guitar player', Calum, volunteered to take on bass guitar duty. In the early days, however, the boys had to improvise, as Ashton explained to *Billboard*: 'Calum didn't even have a bass. He played the top string of an acoustic guitar.' Although it is a similar instrument to the rhythm guitar, playing the bass guitar has a completely different set of rules and skills. A bass-line provides the core of each song's rhythm, working hand-in-hand with the song's beat, supplied by the drummer, and acting as a solid foundation on which a song can be built. Here, in a nutshell, was 5 Seconds' main problem – they didn't have a drummer – and booking gigs without one was looking like a severe case of trying to run before they could walk. Luckily for them, someone had been watching them from afar and was ready and willing to give them the helping hand they desperately needed. 5 Seconds of Summer were about to find that vital, missing ingredient just when they needed it. They were about to find their drummer.

CHAPTER FIVE

ASHTON IRWIN: THE SOUND OF DRUMS

'This band gave me the chance to be a kid again.'
ASHTON IRWIN (@ASHTON5SOS), TWITTER

In 2011, Luke, Michael and Calum were taking their first steps on the path to stardom. Admittedly, at this point their fame was restricted to their families and a few thousand online fans, but those around them were beginning to think there was some real potential in the fledgling band.

They graduated quickly from impromptu gigs at home for their families to playing a handful of small local events. The three boys had become good friends and the boost in confidence they'd experienced after the positive reaction to their first videos pulled them even closer together. The only real problem was that their playing gigs as three singing guitarists was one thing, but it wasn't exactly rock and roll, and it certainly wasn't punk. Their heroes, Blink-182, had never felt the need to expand beyond the core members of Mark Hoppus, Tom DeLonge and Travis Barker, and even Green Day had survived as a trio for many years, but 5 Seconds of Summer really wanted to start their next chapter as a proper four-piece, and that meant vocals, guitars, bass and drums. If it was good enough for The Beatles, it was good enough for 5 Seconds of Summer. They had the guitars, and, with a little re-shuffle, they even had the bass player, but what they really needed was a drummer.

Ashton Fletcher Irwin was born on 7 July 1994 and was raised by his mother, Anne Marie, in the suburb of Hornsby, situated 25 km north-west of Sydney. Unlike Luke, Michael and Calum, he did not study at Norwest College. Rather, Ashton attended non-Christian state school Richmond High, which was a few kilometres further west of his hometown.

His home life was considerably more complicated than his fellow 5SOS band members', as his parents separated when he was still a child, requiring him to take on extra duties at home. He told *Top of the Pops* magazine, 'My parents split when I was younger and, being the oldest, I had to look after my sister … so growing up it was me, my mum and my younger sister – just the three of us until my little brother came along.' This meant Ashton was expected to do more than his fair share of chores, and earned pocket money where he could to help keep the family afloat. In many respects, he was forced to adopt the role of the man of the house at a very early age. While he undoubtedly found life without his father very difficult to begin with, saying it was 'such a big thing to overcome' and that 'it can be scary', he also acknowledges it made him grow up much faster than most, and that in itself was not 'necessarily a bad thing'. Ultimately, the separation from his father only strengthened the close relationship he shared with his mother. It's this bond, she told *60 Minutes*, which remains unbroken wherever his travels now take him, and stops her worrying about her son when he's away from home. 'He texts me every day: "Love you mama". You get that text message, even if it's 3 o'clock in the morning, and then you go back to sleep.'

It is hardly surprising that his advanced maturity and sense of responsibility led him to assume his place as 5 Seconds of Summer's 'father figure'. But rather than being serious or domineering, he is 'the talker and the funny one' of the group, and acts as the leader. Ashton's position in the Irwin household gave him a level-headedness, a stability, and a greater sense of himself – all qualities that would prove invaluable in the fast-moving, unpredictable environment he would later find himself in.

In order to help him explore his love of music and develop his skills as a musician after finishing high school, Ashton decided to attend a local further education college. However, he found it difficult to connect his passion for music with the course work, receiving an F in one of his modules, as he told Sydney's *Sunrise* television show: 'I failed music performance … It was a pretty sad moment really.' Undeterred by his apparent lack of academic prowess, Ashton continued to pursue his dream of being in a successful band, playing with several groups during his early teens and perfecting his drumming skills along the way.

His greatest musical inspiration while growing up was the band Green Day, and he counts hearing their 2005 live album, *Bullet in a Bible*, as one of the most important formative experiences of his teens. He told *Alternative Press*, 'I'm more of a fan of Green Day's live recording. They're amazing.' He would also describe the album, on his official Twitter account, as 'My favourite recording in history. Helped me discover what I wanted to be in life … Rock out and entertain people!'

Ashton was very comfortable in his own skin, his mother said. He inherited self-reliance from her and, from an early age, 'he was confident, he was out there', but, like his future band mates, he still classed himself as a bit of an outsider at school. Perhaps his role as 'semi-parent' to his younger siblings or the lack of spare time he had in his early teens meant he didn't get the chance to form the bonds a child typically makes during their school years. Whatever the reason, he never became one of the 'popular kids', and his experience of dating suffered as a consequence. He described his ideal girl in a *Top of the Pops* interview: 'Character is important, so I look for someone who's confident and interesting.' He recalled that any attempts at pretending to be something he wasn't had failed miserably: 'I've tried to do the whole "cool thing" on a date, but it didn't go down too well.' Ashton would have to wait before he would meet the right kind of girl, one who thought that being the drummer in one of the biggest pop bands in the world *was* cool.

Kendall Jenner, the reality TV star and half-sister to the infamous Kardashian sisters, who had introduced 5 Seconds of Summer at their first major US television appearance at the 2014 *Billboard* Music Awards, was for a time romantically linked with Ashton. The *Mail* Online speculated on the couple's relationship, stating Kendall had been seen 'enjoying a night out in New York with the 5 Seconds of Summer star before they sped off together in a cab'. It would seem unlikely that anything serious was developing between the two, however, as Ashton and Luke told a radio interviewer on the 2Day FM Breakfast Show a few days later: 'You meet people every now and then, but that's sort of like the downside of the job; you don't get to see them every day.' Prior to being linked to Kendall, Ashton had also joked about joining the dating site Tinder, but, like the other members of the band, Ashton would probably have to put any idea of a full-time relationship on hold.

Ashton is the odd one out in the band, having not attended Norwest College and being a bit older than the others, but what is the most surprising fact about him is that before he joined the group, he was by no means a fan of 5 Seconds of Summer. The boys' local celebrity status meant he was well aware of their early videos – he had already checked them out for himself on YouTube – but he was far from impressed. Ashton thought the boys were horsing around too much, forgetting song lyrics and generally needed to take themselves (and the music) more seriously. It's safe to say he'd pretty much written the whole 5SOS thing off as a bit of a joke. When *60 Minutes* asked him if he thought 5 Seconds of Summer needed some help, Ashton replied, 'Of course I did.'

Ashton had already proven to be an accomplished musician – aside from the drums, he can also play piano and guitar – and had started gigging around Sydney with other bands, including as a duo with his friend Blake Green, called Swallow the Goldfish. Their Twitter page, launched in June 2011, described them as 'an acoustic duo from Sydney [who] play original songs as well as all your favourite songs of today's music'. It turned out to be a relatively short-lived project, however, as Ashton was soon being courted by another local band by the name of 5 Seconds of Summer.

5 Seconds still hadn't found the all-important fourth person to fill their vacant drum stool, and with the crucial gig at the Annandale Hotel approaching, the band were desperately looking around for anyone who could help. With little prospect of finding the right drummer through

a conventional audition process, the boys decided to reach out to everyone and anyone they knew who could play the drums. Calum later told Punktastic, 'Michael sent a Facebook message to Ashton who he knew through one of our friends and was like, "Hey man, there's gonna be so many people at the gig we just booked. How would you like to come drum with us?" And Ashton was like, "Hell yeah, that sounds sick!"' If even a small proportion of the band's online following turned up, Ashton calculated that the promise of hundreds of screaming fans wouldn't be too much of an exaggeration, and he was convinced he could iron out any kinks he had noticed in their online performances.

The boys asked him to come down and join them for a few quick, informal practice sessions before the gig. The intention was to hang out, play a few songs and see if they got on. Their first impressions ranged from calling him 'chirpy', to commenting on his 'luscious hair', 'long fingers' and his 'award-winning smile'. Michael jokingly recalled their first meeting in one of the band's online videos: 'We were all judging him because he was wearing a terrible purple shirt.'

Ashton's dubious taste in clothes was the least of his worries. When he said he wasn't interested in playing FIFA and didn't really like computer games in general, it looked like he might fall at the first hurdle. Fortunately, the boys looked past Ashton's lack of enthusiasm for gaming – a particularly difficult blow for Michael – and recognized his skills as a talented drummer. Ashton was a lot more down-to-earth about his feelings towards the other boys, saying, 'I met these guys and everything felt okay. Everybody thinks I'm a bit weird, but these guys like me and I like them and we get along.' No doubt this was the clincher for him.

For now, with this tentative alliance in place, the Annandale gig was on. Despite Michael's boasts of an audience filled with over 200 screaming fans, it didn't quite play out as expected, as Calum explained: 'Twelve people showed up and it was the worst gig that had ever happened' – and one of those twelve was Ashton's mother, who had come along to cheer on her son. However, the boys felt good in each other's presence, and shortly after the gig, as Calum told *Seventeen* magazine, '[I] got down on one knee and proposed to Ashton to be in the band.' With little hesitation, Ashton accepted. It was truly a match made in heaven.

As the starting point for the band, the Annandale gig was fairly inauspicious, but the new drummer felt something special was taking place. 'I remember what we were wearing, the first band photo. We had amazing emo fringes,' Ashton reminisced in *Billboard*. 'I still say it was my favourite gig ever: Magic Day, 3 December 2011.' Appreciating that every great band has to start somewhere, he told the *Sydney Morning Herald*, 'You have to suck at the beginning and you have to have crap for instruments and not be able to afford stuff and work from the bottom for the band to grow.'

It was this mindset, now firmly planted inside the heads of the other boys, which made Ashton the crucial missing ingredient. Almost immediately the dynamic changed within the band, something clicked, and as Calum would later explain, 'Ashton pulled it together a bit more because we started rehearsing properly.' Michael echoed Ashton's importance: 'He was the missing piece of the puzzle. He kind of drove us,' joking, 'Literally, he drove us, because he was the only one who could drive.' The drummer's place as a vital component in the 5SOS success story can never be denied, and being the last to join has not meant he is any less committed to the group than the original members – he even sports a 5SOS logo tattoo to prove it!

With all the pieces now in place, nothing was going to stop 5 Seconds of Summer from bringing their unique brand of do-it-yourself pop-punk to the world. Their musical style may have been out of step with everything contemporary, but they were still determined to do it the way they wanted, every step of the way. Never afraid of hard work, they built from the ground up: four lads willing to do anything to make it a success and with an attitude that said, 'We can do this on our own.' Very quickly, they started to see results, and their commitment to maintaining their online fan base began to pay dividends. As Ashton would later explain to Musictakeabow.com, their method of laying the groundwork in terms of their following made them realize they were at the beginning of a mini-revolution: 'I think it's reversed the music industry in a way. You can build a fan base now before you actually release anything, so it's all quite weird. Whereas before we'd [have to tour] our butts off for, like, years, but that's not the only way that you can build a fan base.' It was a 'punk' way of doing things – no hand-outs, no rules and definitely no limits.

CHAPTER SIX

'BRINGING BACK THE BAND THING'

'When we met, we realised we're the same. We don't necessarily belong.'

ASHTON IRWIN, THE *GUARDIAN*

The gig at the Annandale Hotel was understandably rough around the edges. Ashton described it to *USA Today* as 'a terrible gig', but he was quick to explain why it occupies a very special place in the band's history and why he still counts it as one of his fondest memories of his time with the group. 'It was so new to us … There was something about it that me and the boys loved. We knew it was the start of something cool for us.' Calum also felt the band's instant chemistry and sudden potential, telling *Billboard*, 'We totally sucked, but it just felt right between the four of us on stage.'

With Ashton now on board, the band made an announcement that they had finally found their drummer, and introduced him officially as the newest member of the group. To seal the deal, he joined them on a Ustream chat and they each launched their individual 5SOS Twitter accounts. Within a couple of days, their first video performance as a foursome, a cover of 'Teenage Dirtbag' (originally recorded by Wheatus), was posted on YouTube and shared across the band's other social media accounts. Yet, it still had the same rough-and-ready feel as the previous videos they'd posted as a three-piece, as Ashton explained: 'Everyone else was doing these really clean-cut, amazing edits of popular covers, and we just had an iPhone. We used to wedge it on the mic stand and start filming.' Despite their lack of funding, there was certainly a greater balance as a four-piece. The performance, however, is slightly shambolic. Luke shyly passes on singing the song's (slightly) rude words, but with Ashton beating out the rhythm on a drum box, there is no denying their chemistry and the fact 5 Seconds of Summer finally looked like a proper band. The fans seemed to agree, and the 'Teenage Dirtbag' cover passed 17,000 views in just four days.

The boys took some well-earned time off to enjoy the Christmas holidays, but as 2012 dawned, the creative juices inspired by Ashton's arrival were obviously still flowing, and the new videos kept coming. Over the next few weeks, the boys uploaded covers of All Time Low's 'Jasey Rae' and a medley of One Direction hits, 'What Makes You Beautiful' and 'One Thing'. Yet again, the band were showing the range of their musical tastes and responding well to the frenzied fan requests for them to cover a song by the biggest boy band on the planet.

Elsewhere, their work was starting to get noticed outside of the small, close-knit 5SOS camp. Local radio stations around the world were getting requests to play their music, with one US station, North Carolina's WPLW, boasting, 'We were getting tweets a year before 5 Seconds of Summer even had a major-label deal.' Their impressive social media stats and youthful appeal were also attracting attention from other areas of the music industry, and several record companies approached the band, eager to sign them and take them on to the next level. Thankfully, the boys were savvy enough to know that they were far from ready, still busy deciding exactly what kind of band they wanted to be. They appreciated they had a lot to learn about performing live, and there was also the small matter of finishing school to consider.

Taking it upon themselves to try to brush up on their performance skills, 5SOS were determined to be the best live band they could possibly be. Ashton revealed to Vevo, 'We really worked hard to be a good band. We did everything we could to be a good, credible band.' He outlined the lengths they'd go to in the *Sydney Morning Herald*: 'We did everything. We rehearsed in the dark! We thought if we can't see what we are doing and we can still play then we might sound good when the lights are turned on. We want to be a credible live band so people would come and see us and say, "That's better than we hear on the record."' Michael, realizing how extreme it might appear, added, 'I know it sounds weird, but it worked.' While the boys' early commitment and professionalism was to be commended, it soon became apparent that there was only so much they could do on their own. Even with amazing support from their family and close friends, it was clear the boys needed some professional help.

First thing on the agenda was to get the boys into the recording studio. Previously, while visiting Sydney's Studios 301, Australia's largest studio complex, the boys had a fateful meeting with the studio's manager, Adam Wilkinson. Wilkinson had a long and successful career managing various recording studios before branching out into artist management. At Studios 301 he recorded albums by many local artists, and eventually worked with international acts including Coldplay, Lana Del Rey and Kylie Minogue. In early 2012, he had set up his own management company, AWM Management, and was especially keen to get some fresh young Australian talent on his books. His chance meeting with 5 Seconds of Summer was enough to spark his interest, he told Music Network. 'I immediately liked the look of them and wanted to work with them, but I forgot their name!' Wilkinson continued, 'I took to Facebook and YouTube and finally tracked them down, eventually getting in touch with drummer, Ashton.' Wilkinson joked that the reason Ashton replied was because his message was the only one they'd ever had from a male fan. In the end, Wilkinson signed a co-management deal with the band, sharing duties with Matt Emsell's Wonder Management.

Wilkinson had shared an office with Matt Emsell a couple of years earlier and thought his company had the necessary management experience, but, more importantly, could also offer the boys a more personal, family approach in nurturing their careers. Like Wilkinson, Emsell was an industry veteran, having overseen the early careers of several platinum-selling Australian-based artists, including singer-songwriter Matt Corby, pop-rock band Evermore and pop-punk group Amy Meredith.

With Wilkinson and Emsell now on board, things were stepping up a gear. It was decided that rather than hastily signing a record deal they might regret in the future, they should first sign with a music publisher, someone who could help them make their first moves into writing their own songs and taking control of their own music. They decided to go with Sony/ATV, one of the most respected music publishing companies around, with a huge and diverse repertoire of successful international artists including Beyoncé, Taylor Swift, John Legend, George Michael and Rihanna. Soon, the boys were asking their fans what they wanted to see in the band's merchandise store, they had a professional-looking new band logo and, most exciting of all, they were about to announce their first proper Australian tour.

Matt Emsell was particularly well equipped to help build 5 Seconds of Summer from local phenomenon to major players on the world stage. His theories on building a band's fan base from the ground up had worked spectacularly well with one of his first signings, Evermore, back in the early 2000s. Like 5 Seconds of Summer, Evermore played a blend of pop and rock that appealed to the same young, female audience, and it was this fan base that made up the core of their early gig audiences. Emsell saw the importance of engaging this small but dedicated group of fans, getting them fully involved with the band during their earliest days on the road, telling Startupsmart.com, 'Finding the first ten thousand fans takes careful thought, hard work and patience … After they played, the band would hang around and meet fans, personally selling CD singles and signing them. They met a lot of people in two years and these fans felt special … They'd seen a show, had met the band personally and became evangelists, calling their local radio stations requesting the songs. Momentum started to build.' That momentum would eventually deliver Evermore a couple of platinum-selling albums and a string of hit songs between 2004 and 2009.

With the head start the 5SOS boys already had, their building up of a fan base was going to be a little easier, with the evangelical core already in place. The band's insistence on staying in close contact with their fans via their social media profiles was now bearing fruit, as Ashton pointed out: 'We pay attention to our online fans and they really give it back. They share our stuff and they are really coming on the journey.' The group was well aware this type of unrestricted access might lead to a loss of mystique and privacy, however. Ashton continued, 'It's not the eighties anymore and we're not a mysterious rock star. People know everything we do.' But Michael was quick to tell MusicFeeds.com just how much the attention meant to them: 'We get fans coming up to us wherever we go now … it's a pretty surreal feeling for us boys, because we're still in school and still do all the normal stuff, just like other teenagers … We love our fans so much, though, and we are so grateful to have such a dedicated fan base.'

Emsell's plans for engaging with the fans extended to how the band is presented during those all-important first live shows. 'No one likes to hang out in an empty bar, no matter how great the music is. The best way to experience a new band is in a small venue crammed with screaming fans – a small group of trendy tastemakers who will be the first in the world to discover this great talent … Then one day they can say, "I saw them at venue X with two hundred other people and now they're playing stadiums."'

With this theory in mind, the band was scheduled to play three dates in Sydney, Melbourne and Brisbane in relatively small locations, each with the capacity to hold 200 to 300 people. On the day of the pre-sale, the gigs sold out in minutes, with the press reporting that the online ticketing sites for each venue had crashed due to the exceptional demand. The boys announced a second show at each of the venues, and these too sold out within minutes of going on sale. 5 Seconds of Summer were officially on their way, with their first sold-out tour under their belt.

Having penned only a few original songs at this point, the boys had to decide which of their many covers they were going to record. Studio time was booked for 21 April, and the boys took their baby steps into a much bigger world. The first track they recorded together in a professional studio was 'I Miss You', the Blink-182 song that had become a firm favourite not only with the band, but also among the fans. This single stands as the perfect example of the boys' willingness to reflect on their output and attempt to rediscover and rework music that may be completely new to many of their young following – after all, Blink-182's version of 'I Miss You' was originally released when Luke was just seven years old.

In early May 2012, an American website, the Hot Hits, gave the band their first international write-up, raving about them and labelling them as 'the band you should be obsessing over'. Back in Australia, no one really needed the heads-up, and as the band's live dates loomed, the fans' excitement was reaching fever pitch. The boys gave their first ever interview to MusicFeeds.com, with Ashton, as ever the spokesperson, discussing their rapid progress and teasing their future plans. 'We've only really been a band for four months, but we are hoping to begin working on our debut release of original stuff as soon as possible … We've got a bunch of writing sessions coming up and we're rehearsing a few times a week and writing all the time. We really just want to get it right for our fans and give them something they want. We're all pretty excited, though … Everything is coming together slowly but surely.'

Recording continued, and soon the idea of releasing their first EP to satisfy the demands of their ever-growing fan base was all the boys could think about. They knew the EP would have to feature at least a couple of the songs performed in their early videos, but as they told the *Daily Telegraph*, 'We want people to respect us as musicians rather than a YouTube covers band.' To get the credibility they craved, they needed to push on with writing their own material. Their confidence as songwriters had grown, but they realized they still lacked some of the skills necessary to create songs that matched the quality of the covers they'd already recorded. Manager Matt Emsell and the boys agreed that they needed to collaborate with other artists in the writing process, and the decision was taken to start looking around for co-writers for 5 Seconds to work and record with. Luckily, Emsell had another similarly rock-orientated group based in Sydney on his books, who also just happened to be signed to Sony/ATV Publishing. Soon the 5SOS boys found themselves locked away with the creative songwriting team behind rock band Amy Meredith.

Singer Christian Lo Russo, along with Joel Chapman, Cameron Laing and Wade Osborn, had come together to form Amy Meredith in 2006. They had enjoyed moderate success after being signed to Sony Australia, scoring a Top

10 album. When their deal with Sony came to an end, the band decided to sign with an independent company instead, hoping it would give them more creative freedom and the chance to experiment and expand their sound. Part of that willingness to explore new creative outlets would see different members of the band working with several outside writers and artists, including the boys from 5 Seconds of Summer. Everyone involved in the Amy Meredith camp embraced the idea of aiding a group of talented, but inexperienced, young musicians find their own musical direction and relished the chance to help tutor them in the art of songwriting, as well as giving the band the benefit of their experience in the recording studio.

It was a very successful pairing, opening the boys up to the world of a professional musician and providing them with a solid grounding in the writing and recording process. Over the course of the next few months, the 5SOS boys met with members of Amy Meredith on numerous occasions, writing and recording a number of songs. One track, 'Beside You' – written by Lo Russo and Chapman, with Luke and Calum – surfaced first as part of the *Somewhere New* EP, and was later re-recorded to become the oldest song written by the band to appear on their debut album, almost two years later. This song was a particular favourite, with Ashton telling HMV's website, 'We always loved it and it sort of got buried [on the *Somewhere New* EP]. We didn't want to waste it, so we wanted to redo it.'

This was a very special time for the group, opening them up to new experiences and allowing them to fully express themselves creatively for the first time. Ashton recalled how significant these first sessions had been: 'I remember travelling three hours by train in Australia to write with Amy Meredith – you remember the songs you listened to on the train, everything.'

Just ahead of the tour, the boys decided it was time to give their faithful supporters a little taste of what they'd been working on over the last few months. On 21 May, they unveiled the video for their first original song, 'Gotta Get Out'. A solo writing outing for Calum, with its mid-tempo, breezy rhythm and infectious harmonies, 'Gotta Get Out' is a confident first step for the band, and the song's bittersweet lyrics are surprisingly mature and heartfelt. The video is of course a far more professional affair than any of their previous efforts, with multiple camera angles, close-ups and a much higher quality finish. The boys were extremely proud of their efforts and their confidence as performers was noticeably growing in front of the camera.

The tour began with two dates at Sydney's Factory Theatre on 25 and 26 May, and the boys had ensured the audience was whipped into a frenzy of excitement, with frequent countdowns to the gigs employed across social media platforms and several chances to directly interact with the band. They launched a fan art competition, with the best entrants winning a merchandise pack and the opportunity to attend one of the organized meet and greets that would take place at each venue. Such a close connection to the band during the early stages of their career virtually guaranteed the unquestioning loyalty of the growing 5SOS family, who felt a valued part of the continuing 5 Seconds story. Even a last-minute change of venue for the Melbourne shows, as the advertised location was forced to close, failed to derail the unstoppable 5SOS Express, and the rest of the tour flew by in a whirlwind of excitement and adrenalin. To celebrate the success of their live shows, the band created an online poster featuring photos submitted by the fans, encouraging their followers to tag themselves and share the pictures.

As the tour came to an end, 5 Seconds of Summer were trending worldwide on Twitter. Still six months away from marking their first year together as a band, it was clear things were moving in the right direction, and the rest of the world was beginning to take notice of the four teenagers from Sydney.

Soon the official 5SOS online merchandise store opened for business, initially selling the T-shirts the band had produced for the Australian tour dates. It then expanded to sell the boys' own designs as limited editions, as well as 5SOS baseball and beanie hats and countless other accessories.

Another set of live dates was announced, and this time the 'Twenty Twelve Tour' would take the group further afield as they visited Adelaide, as well as the cities they had played previously, during late July and early August. Unsurprisingly, the Sydney and Brisbane shows sold out within hours, and tickets were going fast for the rest of the tour.

More studio time was booked, and, as the finishing touches were made, the band announced the release of their first official extended play. The *Unplugged* EP would consist of two original songs, 'Gotta Get Out' and 'Too Late', as well as two covers, 'I Miss You' and All Time Low's 'Jasey Rae'. The inclusion of the two covers, both of which had previously appeared in early YouTube videos, were fitting reminders of how far the boys had come, showing a remarkable progression in their musical abilities, as well as the developing sophistication and maturity in their performance.

At the last instant, the release of the EP was delayed by one week, with the band posting an elaborate story on Facebook involving Mount Everest, a bear and sending Calum to retrieve the EP, by way of an apology. It also gently reminded everyone that their first official release would be available to buy from iTunes on 26 July 2012.

Sitting comfortably alongside new albums from Maroon 5, Justin Bieber, Katy Perry and Lady Gaga, the 5 Seconds of Summer *Unplugged* EP was highlighted in the iTunes store, and sales got off to a strong start. With no major record company behind them and no marketing team to publicize the EP, the boys had to do most of the work themselves. They promoted the release with a week-long series of meet and greets and signing sessions, Ustream chats and several high-profile media interviews – including a live acoustic performance on radio station Nova FM and a piece in one of Australia's most popular tabloid newspapers, the *Daily Telegraph*. This grass-roots approach proved to be extremely successful, and their legion of fans were keen to show their support.

The single peaked at Number Three in the Australian iTunes chart and climbed inside the Top 20 in the official Australian and New Zealand charts, as well as becoming a hit in Sweden. A remarkable achievement for anyone's first single, and all the more extraordinary when one considers it was self-released.

Confidence was growing within the band and the management team. It was clear everyone around the boys were beginning to believe 5 Seconds of Summer had the potential to go all the way, not only as major players on the Australian music scene, but around the world, too. As the band's Facebook followers passed the 50,000 mark, it looked like Matt Emsell's masterplan was becoming a reality: 5 Seconds of Summer were no longer just four normal teenagers who shared the dream of starting their own band; they were becoming a global hit, and as yet it was unclear where this journey would end up.

On the other side of the world, in One Direction's London headquarters, reports were filtering through about a new pop band who had just charted their first single, created their own worldwide following and were about to start their second headlining tour of Australia – all without a major record deal. Calum explained how hugely significant One Direction member Louis Tomlinson's interest in his band was, telling Punktastic, 'Louis found us on YouTube and was like, "We should do something with this band."' Calls were made, and soon the idea was floated that 5 Seconds of Summer could be the perfect group to join One Direction as the main support act on their next world tour. With the management team of Emsell, and especially Wilkinson, pulling out all the stops to make the deal happen, it was an exciting time for everyone associated with the band. Michael explained just how much of a fantasy it all seemed: 'When the guys first started talking to us about it, we thought they were joking.'

By the time negotiations were being made, the boys were already on the road themselves, about to embark on their Twenty Twelve Tour. Calum recalled, 'In Adelaide, we were having lunch and we had this piece of paper that was put in front of us telling us we were doing a world tour and listing all the venues, and it was just endless pieces of paper. Mindblowing.'

Things were undoubtedly moving fast, with each successive milestone adding even more momentum to the 5 Seconds of Summer machine. But the boys were struggling to keep up with their studies and stay focused on their 'real lives' at home. It was only going to get worse, as more and more of their free time was swallowed up by band practices, meeting fans and the rest of their new commitments. As Luke told the Music Feeds website, 'We're all still trying to juggle this with school, but we're making it work as best we can.'

Unfortunately, it wasn't just their school lives that were suffering under the strain of the added pressure. Luke's relationship with his girlfriend came to an end in August, with a heartbroken Aleisha posting on her Facebook page, 'Today has successfully earned its position as the worst day of my life.' It would appear the pair decided to break up amicably, undoubtedly as a consequence of Luke's increasingly hectic schedule. Luke's feelings for Aleisha apparently remained as strong as ever, though. When he was asked by a fan in a Twitter question and answer session a few months later to name the best thing that had happened in his life besides 5SOS, he replied, 'Probably my ex-girlfriend.'

With a little over six months to go before the start of the One Direction tour, the decision to put the band first had been made by all four lads – there was a lot of work to do to ensure they were completely ready for the challenge ahead. There could be no distractions and they needed to concentrate 100 per cent on the band, and with that, they got their heads down and got to work. They needed to keep rehearsing if they wanted to get their live show up to scratch and they required more material for their set list. They had no intention of touring the world playing only a bunch of other people's songs.

The writing sessions with Amy Meredith had gone extremely well and had helped clarify the boys' own ideas as to what direction they wanted to take the band musically. Keen to find more co-writers to help them build a varied catalogue of original material, with a view to releasing another EP of new songs and eventually their first album, the word went out to several potential writing partners, and this time the net was thrown far and wide.

The boys were beginning to put into place the sound they wanted going forward. Ashton explained to Vevo, 'We all were brought up in the time of Green Day ... and that type of music has just influenced us so much today.' Luke confirmed the importance of another successful US rock group, Good Charlotte, to their masterplan: '[They] are the reason I started playing guitar. That's kind of why all of us started, bands like that.'

While it's true that in the decade between 1995 and 2005 bands such as Green Day, Blink-182 and Good Charlotte were big players on the international music scene, none of them had been particularly interested in attracting massive pop audiences in the same way as their contemporaries the Spice Girls, *NSYNC and the Backstreet Boys. Therefore, at the time, none of them fully crossed over into an area where they might also attract a much younger, female audience – the fan base that 5 Seconds of Summer already seemed to have hooked. Pointing out how things had moved on from the origins of the pop-punk boom in the early 2000s, record producer John Feldmann – one of the boys' eventual collaborators – noted in an interview with *Billboard* in

August 2014, 'In the first wave of Green Day and Blink-182, [the crowd was] ninety-eight per cent dudes ... Now, I would say it's eighty per cent girls.'

It was clear the boys' decision to continue down the road signposted by their earliest musical influences was a shrewd one, but they also didn't want to be a carbon copy of their heroes. Some elements of their beloved pop-punk didn't sit well with their masterplan, as Ashton would later tell *Alternative Press*. 'If there's one thing I hate about pop-punk, it's people thinking you have to do the whole [double-time] thing ... I think it's a bit ugly ... I was raised on that. When I'd go to pubs and see bands like that, I'd just think, "Slow down!"'

Instead, they wanted to refine, adapt and update the sound of these groups for today's audience, as Michael explained: 'We're kind of like a big lovechild of all our influences. We take pop influences to stay modern because ultimately we wanna modernize nineties and early 2000s rock with nowadays pop.' While it was this pop element the boys were especially keen to blend, knowing it would appeal to their existing fans, they didn't want to dilute the essence of the band – they were real musicians who played their own instruments – and the thought of being handed songs to perform by a team of faceless producers was never a scenario they wanted to buy into. Although they respected other groups who represented the more traditional 'all singing, all dancing pop boy band' – they had, after all, covered both

One Direction and the Backstreet Boys – they wanted to be known for their musical skills and writing their own songs. Calum succinctly summed it up by telling Vevo they wanted to 'bring back the whole band thing'.

It was certainly the tougher route. While the guitar-led, pop-punk sound had fallen slightly out of favour in the last few years, replaced in the mainstream charts by a succession of more polished R&B, dance and pop artists, rock music was still thriving. A new breed of more sophisticated sounding rock bands were flourishing, especially in the US, inspiring many young musicians (including the 5SOS boys) to pick up guitars and start their own groups. Bands like All Time Low, Mayday Parade and A Day To Remember were breaking through from the underground and beginning to achieve widespread commercial acceptance. What the boys from 5 Seconds of Summer began to realize was, if they could combine the separate strands of pop, rock and punk music together, they would have a winning formula that would tap into a huge gap in the market.

While a few credible and successful pop-rock crossover tracks, such as Kelly Clarkson's 'Since U Been Gone' and Pink's 'So What', had been created with the help of studio-based pop producers, the artist's involvement would vary from case to case. Finding seasoned writers willing to sit down, sometimes for weeks on end, with such inexperienced singers and bands to help them shape their own ideas into songs might be a tall order. Fortunately, there was one place where this experimental mash-up of genres had already succeeded, a place that was also home to a disproportionate number of like-minded songwriters. Almost ten years earlier, a young band named Busted had made it big in the UK with a similarly energetic blend of pop-punk and rock. The 5 Seconds of Summer boys were about to find some kindred spirits half way around the world, in London, England.

It had transpired that several established British songwriters and production teams, including Busted's James Bourne and McFly's Tom Fletcher, had expressed an interest in meeting with Luke, Michael, Calum and Ashton. They were not only available, but very keen to have an input in the emerging 5 Seconds of Summer sound. A plan was hatched to send the boys on a two-week songwriting trip to London, in the hope that the proposed collaborations might work well enough for them to return to Australia with the majority of their debut album written and ready to record. A trip to London might also give them a chance to meet their soon-to-be tour-mates, One Direction, and get the finer details of that particular contract worked out.

So, at the end of August 2012, the day after the boys played a free acoustic gig in Sydney's Hyde Park, they told their fans that they would be heading to London in less than a month's time. Ahead of the trip, the band hinted at the reason for their long-distance travels, uploading a video of them performing Busted's 'Year 3000'. They also made several other announcements about their immediate schedule, including their first show outside Australia – they would play a single date in New Zealand on 3 November – but most impressive of all was that, shortly after their return from London, thanks to another deal struck by Wilkinson, they would be joining US rock band Hot Chelle Rae and their support act, UK *X Factor* finalist Cher Lloyd, on the Australian leg of their current tour. Although they were all cities the band had played before, these were by far their biggest gigs to date.

The London trip was an amazing opportunity for the foursome, one that would have seemed unimaginable a few months earlier. It was particularly exciting for Luke, who had never before been outside of Australia.

First on the agenda was setting up a small acoustic show in London's Hyde Park. The boys were desperate to meet their fans from half way around the world and invited them to come along to the performance on Twitter and Facebook. It seems extraordinary anyone would turn up at all, considering the boys were based thousands of miles away on a different continent and had not yet released any music for their British fans to buy, but an enthusiastic group of about fifty turned up to hear a few songs and chat to the boys.

During the remainder of their London adventure, the group would go on to meet some of the UK's most established songwriters and firm up their important new business connections, setting the wheels in motion for what was about to become the craziest time of their lives so far. Just prior to leaving the UK and heading home, as a 'thank you' to the British fans, they uploaded a cover of Ed Sheeran's 'Give Me Love', live from their London base. The gesture served to highlight how far their social media activities had brought them, geographically and figuratively.

The boys returned to Australia suitably fired up. Their London trip had helped them develop and flex more of their creative muscles, and with growing self-belief they continued writing and recording with Christian and Joel from Amy Meredith as they inched closer to releasing their next EP. By the end of October, with the Hot Chelle Rae dates under their belts, the boys added the finishing touches to the new songs they had recorded, and announced to their eager fans that they would be releasing the *Somewhere New* EP in the first week of December.

What they couldn't have known was that their world was about to be turned on its head. One message, containing only thirteen words, was about to become the most important piece of promotion they would ever receive, and it would change their lives forever.

CHAPTER SEVEN

LONDON CALLING

'London. So cold!!!'

5 SECONDS OF SUMMER, FACEBOOK

The tweet, sent on 6 November 2012, read, 'Been a fan of this band for a while, everyone get behind them,' and included a link to the YouTube video for 'Gotta Get Out'. While 5 Seconds had received many similarly encouraging messages in the last year, this had been sent from the Twitter account of Louis Tomlinson, one fifth of One Direction, the biggest boy band in the world.

The story behind the two groups' relationship is fascinating. It is said Louis had found the band's video for 'Teenage Dirtbag' on YouTube some time earlier. It must have made quite an impression, and was certainly enough to inspire him to investigate further. Perhaps intrigued by reports of the young Australian pop band who had already covered one of his own band's songs, it had led him to find the more polished and professional sounding 'Gotta Get Out'. Instantly hooked, Louis was soon championing 5 Seconds of Summer among his fellow band mates and alerted the 1D management team about their potential. In what seemed like a blink of an eye, 5 Seconds of Summer had been suggested as a possible support act for their tour, and the wheels were set in motion. By the time of the famous tweet, negotiations had been going on behind the scenes for some time, but with the tour only a matter of months away and unable to keep his discovery under wraps any longer, it would seem Louis wanted to let his Twitter followers see for themselves what all the fuss was about. That Twitter audience – which currently sits at just under 17 million followers – was suitably impressed, and soon the video had over 75,000 retweets.

In today's world, something as simple as a tweet can become the most powerful piece of promotion any recording artist could ever receive – especially if that tweet comes from a member of one of the most popular bands in the world. The effect of Louis's thirteen words was instantaneous and unprecedented. The band's YouTube views, Facebook 'Likes' and Twitter followers started to increase exponentially.

Suddenly, the band was in the global spotlight like never before: invitations to play shows came flooding in and the level of media attention was astounding. Soon it seemed the world of social media couldn't stop talking about 5 Seconds of Summer, either.

The team that looked after and managed the group was completely stunned by the scale of what had happened, and a decision was taken to hold off from officially announcing the band's spot on the One Direction tour for as long as possible. It was hard enough to take Louis's tweet in, let alone the reaction following it. Every attempt would be made to shield 5 Seconds of Summer from the glare of the world's press and media, especially during a period when they were still trying to maintain a regular existence outside of the band, with school, exams and a normal life at home with their families still all-important. It became everyone's priority to keep the boys' feet firmly on the ground. The time had come for some very serious conversations involving the boys and their parents; they all had big decisions to make about their futures, both short-term and long-term.

A year or so before, when the boys had told them they wanted to make music professionally, their parents had reacted with surprise. As Calum told radio station KIIS 1065, 'They were kind of like, "Why would you want to join a band?"' The parents had initially turned a blind eye to late homework assignments and escalating demands on their sons' time due to band commitments, but soon they grew increasingly concerned about their children's future prospects, fearful and sceptical about their chances, at such a young age, of finding a stable career in the famously fickle and cutthroat music industry. It had been a stressful few months as the mothers and fathers stood back, watching the boys desperately juggle their personal lives with their parallel lives as budding rock stars. But as the band's confidence grew, and their parents began to see how committed they were, any doubts turned into fervent support, Ashton revealing, 'They had faith for some reason and they really got behind it in the end.'

5 Seconds of Summer were now generating serious heat within a music industry fascinated by their impressive social media statistics and keen to get in on the action. While interest in them was only increasing, as a band, they still felt relatively inexperienced. The pressure was on to sign a record deal, but the boys decided they would rather take more time to build their stockpile of original songs and work on their stage chemistry to get their live performances as tight as possible. If anything was going to give them the opportunity to grow as a band, it was performing every night to a packed stadium on a 100-date tour of the world's biggest cities. Luckily for them, while their upturn in fortunes may have ramped up the pressure, it also presented them with the confidence to not rush into anything. Alongside the amazing opportunities they'd already been given, the boys decided to embark on another songwriting and recording trip to London, this time for an extended period ahead of the One Direction tour.

While the boys' parents were fully supportive of their sons' ongoing involvement with the band, an extended trip overseas would mean they would effectively be away from home for much of the next twelve months, a huge step up in terms of commitment to the group's future. At this point, only Michael had officially left high school; Luke and Calum were still enrolled at Norwest, undoubtedly struggling to stay on top of their studies, and Ashton had left Richmond and finished his exams at the college. It was make or break time for all of them. Luke and Calum would have to drop out of school before they had the chance to graduate if they wanted to join the other members of the band in London and on the 1D tour. After much soul-searching, all four members of the group decided they wanted to continue with 5 Seconds of Summer. Reviewing the ground they'd managed to cover in just a year, and their seemingly unlimited potential, it all added up to too great an opportunity to throw away at the first real obstacle.

Before heading to London, there was the small matter of releasing their first proper EP, *Somewhere New*. It would contain their first set of completed studio recordings, including lead song 'Out Of My Limit', two tracks – 'Beside You' and 'Unpredictable' – that were written during their sessions with Amy Meredith, as well as a version of 'Gotta Get Out'. Throughout late November and early December, the band teased artwork, posted pictures of the CDs as they arrived at the 5SOS headquarters, revealed their first proper music video (for 'Out Of My Limit') and eventually launched the single by playing a special hometown show at the Metro

Theatre in Sydney. Three days before the EP's release, the band were on their way to London.

It was almost exactly a year since the boys played their first gig as a four-piece, and they couldn't help but reflect on how far they'd come and their decision to leave school and commit to the band full-time. Later, Luke told Connecticut radio station, 96.5 TIC FM, 'We're still really young ... we had to grow up a lot, really quick in the space of a year. It was a big step for us boys, but we're proud.' Undeniably, they had plenty to be proud of. Undoubtedly the London trip was going to be the icing on the cake.

On arriving, the boys quickly settled into the apartment that was to be their home for the next few months. Split over two floors, it was a modern, newly furnished flat – so new, in fact, that it didn't have a television or Wi-Fi. There were two separate bedrooms, with Michael and Ashton choosing to share one, and Luke and Calum the other. Ashton was quick to stamp his own style on his room, making sure his bed was fully decked out with a leopard print duvet cover.

The first couple of days were spent getting used to their new surroundings, with trips to the nearby malls to buy supplies for their London stay. The weather in England was a rude awakening for the boys, with heavy snowfalls and freezing temperatures – was it just a coincidence that a range of 5SOS jumpers went on sale in the merchandise store during their time in the city? It wasn't all going to be fun and games, however. They had a lot of work to do before the tour, and within days they found themselves getting stuck into the job at hand – there was an album's worth of songs to write and record, after all.

The boys had scheduled a number of meetings with respected songwriters and musicians, and less than a week after their arrival were already hard at work at Chewdio, the East London recording studio owned and run by former Kaiser Chiefs drummer Nick Hodgson. Nick had only announced his departure from the band the week before, coincidentally the same day the 5SOS boys arrived in London, but it was by no means a spur-of-the-moment decision. He had been a founding member of Kaiser Chiefs, playing the drums and becoming one of the key songwriters throughout their fifteen-year career, and had made the decision some time earlier to quit the band once he turned thirty-five. Although the rest of the Kaisers were sad to see him go, the split was amicable, with the band's lead singer, Ricky Wilson, tweeting a message of support and stating he was always welcome to rejoin the band at any point in the future. The boys were thrilled to be working alongside a proper musician, with Ashton no doubt particularly excited to spend some time behind the drum kit alongside such an experienced fellow drummer.

5 Seconds also spent time writing and recording with Roy Stride, the main songwriter for English indie-rock band Scouting for Girls. Roy had been responsible for writing every song on his band's breakthrough debut album, as well as its

follow-up. Both of these records charted in the Top 3 in the UK, with combined sales of over a million copies, and would provide the boys with the help they needed in bridging the pop-rock divide.

As well as Stride and Hodgson, the boys had the opportunity to work with Rick Parkhouse and George Tizzard, songwriters for production team Red Triangle, who were behind recent hits by Olly Murs, Pixie Lott, Little Mix and Cheryl Cole, and veteran writer-producer Richard Stannard, the man who co-wrote 'Wannabe' for the Spice Girls and went on to score countless hits with a wide range of pop acts, including Kylie Minogue, Five, Westlife, Will Young, and a more recent collaboration with Ellie Goulding on her track, 'Lights'. These sessions proved especially fruitful, with several of the songs that had their origins in this period finding their way onto various future releases, including 'Lost Boy', 'Close As Strangers', 'Greenlight' and 'Voodoo Doll', with 'English Love Affair', 'Good Girls' and '18' eventually featuring on the standard twelve-track version of the boys' debut album.

Perhaps the most important connection the boys made during this period was Steve Robson, a seasoned British songwriter and producer with a long and varied career in the music industry. Robson had been influential in pop-rock band Busted's success, refining their sound over extensive writing and recording sessions to ultimately help them create something distinctly their own. Robson was aware all three members of Busted were extremely talented individuals, each with a similar dream to the one 5 Seconds of Summer shared – like Luke, Michael, Calum and Ashton, they wanted to write their own songs and have a major stake in their band's output. Robson was determined to nurture Busted's creativity and, with his help, the three-piece were encouraged to contribute to every one of the songs that would eventually make up their self-titled debut album and its sequel. Both records peaked at Number Two in the UK album charts, selling close to 1 million copies each.

A little-known fact at the time, but well publicized since, was that Busted had a secret weapon. It was revealed that a key element in their success story had been the songwriting talents of unofficial fourth member, Tom Fletcher. Tom had auditioned unsuccessfully to join the band, having just been beaten to the job by Charlie Simpson, but had stayed in touch with the boys, eventually co-writing almost half the tracks on the band's second album, mostly in partnership with group member Bourne. Tom decided he wanted a piece of the action and formed his own band, McFly, in 2003. The relationship Tom already had with Busted proved invaluable. Busted invited McFly out on tour with them, and the new group eventually signed a record deal with the same label, Island Records. McFly's initial success even outstripped their mentor's, clocking up fifteen consecutive Top 10 singles and five Top 10 albums in the UK between 2004 and 2008. Neither band managed to make much of a splash in America, but both acts did score a couple of hits in Australia and New Zealand.

McFly's combined worldwide album sales are in excess of 11 million at the time of writing, and both bands still enjoy a solid following thanks to the creation of McBusted – a mash-up of McFly and Busted featuring all four members of the former with Matt Willis and James from the latter – touring and playing one-off gigs throughout 2014.

The differences between the early careers of 5SOS and those of Busted and McFly are fairly obvious – the 5SOS boys did not have the backing of a major player like Island Records – but the similarities are equally striking. Musically, both bands seemed to fit neatly into the commercial pop-punk category the 5SOS lads were aiming for, and parallels can be found in their desire to be fully involved creatively in the writing and recording of their own music.

With his involvement in shaping the sound of Busted, which subsequently led to the success of McFly, Steve Robson looked like the perfect match for the boys. Equally important was that in the years following his involvement with Busted, Robson had continued working at the highest level, writing and producing numerous hit songs for some of the UK's biggest pop artists, such as Take That, Olly Murs, One Direction and Leona Lewis. Robson enjoys a unique position in his field, displaying enormous versatility and an ability to lend his talents to a wide range of artists, having also worked with singer-songwriters James Blunt and James Morrison, as well as having a profitable sideline in writing songs for some of Nashville's biggest country stars, following the enormous success of his song 'What Hurts the Most' when it was covered by Rascal Flatts in 2006. Was there really anyone better equipped to understand what makes a hit record, or so able to navigate the ins and outs of today's ever-evolving music industry?

With a wealth of experience and a genuine love of all types of music, here was someone perfectly placed to understand what 5 Seconds wanted and who could help make it a reality. He knew exactly where to take the boys' emerging sound, after smoothing off some of their rougher edges while still leaving their raw energy intact. Robson was a real inspiration to the band, not only as a mentor in the studio, but also by giving them exceptional support during what must have been an intense period in their lives. Despite the amount of work they had to do, he managed to keep the atmosphere fun as well as creative, and Michael was quick to acknowledge they appreciated what an opportunity they had been given by coming to London. He told the *Daily Telegraph*, 'It's pretty cool to work with people whose music you have listened to and loved.' He also commented specifically on the significance of working alongside Robson: 'He's done heaps so that was a pretty big deal … I have asked him for a bunch of stories because he did Busted and they are one of my favourite bands … He was the coolest dude.' This partnership would significantly shape the development of the band's overall sound and resulted in the creation of 'The Only Reason', and eventual key album tracks 'Heartbreak Girl' and 'Don't Stop', the latter giving 5 Seconds of Summer their second consecutive Top 3 hit in the UK in May 2014.

With the One Direction support slot news still firmly under wraps, the boys were keen to let the fans know that they were still very much on their minds, even if they were half way around the world. They decided that releasing a track, written and recorded during their time in London, would let their most loyal fans know exactly what they'd been up to while they'd been away. 'Heartbreak Girl' was teased from the beginning of February, before finally being made available as a free download on the thirteenth. They posted a special message on their Facebook page saying, 'This is one of the songs we've been working on in London and we wanted you to be the first to hear it!! We're proud of it, and we hope you like it too … This is for you.'

While the boys were working hard in various studios and recording rooms around London, behind the scenes the final negotiations were falling into place, and the deal was finally sealed that would ensure the boys' lives would never be the same. Luke, Michael, Calum and Ashton were ready to make their big announcement – it was time to let the world in on their little secret.

On Valentine's Day 2013, they announced to all their supporters around the world that they were about to join one of the most popular bands in the world, on one of the biggest arena tours of the year: as the very special guests of One Direction. 5 Seconds of Summer were now about to hit the big time.

CHAPTER EIGHT

NEW DIRECTION

'Where can we find the largest number of teen-age girls in the world? We can find them at a One Direction concert. That's who's going to buy our record, so we should go and play to them.'
NICK RAPHAEL, PRESIDENT OF CAPITOL RECORDS
UK, *MUSIC WEEK*

When the band stated, '2013 is going to be the biggest year ever! We love you all!' in their New Year message to their Facebook followers, it certainly wasn't an understatement. No doubt they were keen to drop a few hints about their soon-to-be-revealed plans, preparing everyone for the next major developments in the 5 Seconds of Summer story. In retrospect, the plan to move the boys to London at the end of 2012 probably had as much to do with the deal being worked out with One Direction as with getting the boys on another working trip to continue writing tracks for the debut album. It seems only natural that on their extended stay in London they would get the chance to meet 1D, a necessity in order to make sure everyone got along before rehearsals for the tour began in earnest. It would also give them the chance to get themselves mentally and physically prepared for the challenge ahead.

As it turned out, everything came together perfectly, and the 5SOS boys managed to spend plenty of time getting to know One Direction. Niall Horan had found the opportunity to hang out with them at a studio session in January, and the rest of the 1D lads also extended the challenge of a football match – one that reportedly ended with 5 Seconds being resoundingly thrashed 15 to 2.

As well as beginning a solid relationship with One Direction, the boys made some very important contacts within the music industry, writing and recording several new songs – some finished, and the initial groundwork laid for several more – before preparations for their next big adventure got fully underway. The boys had some adjustments to make: they were about to see the world as the support act for the biggest boy band on the planet and meet millions of new fans. They had certainly come a long way from the Norwest College music room.

One Direction had found enormous popularity around the world in one of the most extraordinary, and rapid, success stories in recent history. Their origins were fairly humble, having been put together by Simon Cowell and his team for the 2010 season of *The X Factor* – the UK's biggest reality singing competition – after each of the five lads had auditioned and then ultimately been rejected as solo singers at the Boot Camp stage. With the show's group category lacking strong contenders, the producers decided to build a boy band themselves using some of the unlucky solo artists. Thus Harry Styles, Zayn Malik, Louis Tomlinson, Niall Horan and Liam Payne became One Direction, and the rest is history.

Although the band failed to win the show (they actually came third behind winner Matt Cardle and runner-up Rebecca Ferguson), it was the clear from the crowd's reactions during the *X Factor* arena tour that followed the series that One Direction were going to be big. Using social media to connect with a huge, worldwide following without releasing a single note of music – although they contributed to the *X Factor* finalists' charity release, 'Heroes', their winner's single, 'Forever Young', remained unreleased after the show – their fans would have a long wait before 'What Makes You Beautiful' finally became their debut release, almost a full year after the band sang in their first live show.

One Direction had already toured extensively following the release of their debut album, *Up All Night*. It had seen them travel all around the world, taking them to America for the first time, and even saw them playing a handful of dates in Australia. In all, they played more than fifty shows in eight countries, across three different continents, keeping the boys on the road for nearly six months to the beginning of July 2012. One Direction's success was in overdrive, with more and more countries falling under their spell.

The momentum was unstoppable as they geared up to release their second album in less than a year. Titled *Take Me Home,* the record would see them score their second Number One in America – becoming the first boy band to hit the US top spot twice in the same year with two different albums – and the tour planned to support it needed to reflect the massive growth in their worldwide popularity. The Take Me Home Tour would consist of almost twice as many dates, expanding the number of American and Australian shows, as well as taking the boys across Europe and to Japan for the first time. From February 2013 until the beginning of November, they planned to visit twenty-one countries in all, making it one of the longest and most extensive pop tours of all time.

There had been eight support acts playing on different legs of the Up All Night Tour. They had been mostly up-and-coming artists, and some of them had been specifically picked by the band after finding their songs on YouTube or having been recommended by people in their management team. For the Take Me Home Tour, they were looking for just one exciting new band to join them for most of the dates, and 5 Seconds of Summer were the perfect fit. 1D's Niall Horan explained, 'We discovered 5SOS on YouTube last year, and we all knew straight away they were very special. We're so excited to have them on the road with us and we know our fans are going to LOVE what these lads do.'

While the opportunity on offer to 5 Seconds was obviously beyond any of their wildest dreams, there were a lot of serious discussions to be had and important decisions to be made – and they had to be made fast.

From the moment the tour was suggested, everyone involved in 5 Seconds of Summer's career realized it would give them the chance to play to millions of people who had probably never heard their music before – invaluable exposure for any band trying to break through. Initially, the only concern the boys had was if the One Direction audience would understand and accept the music 5 Seconds of Summer were committed to playing. 1D play pure pop, after all, and 5SOS's guitar-driven pop-punk might just be a step too far for the average Directioner. As Steve Barnett, US head of the boys' future label, Capitol, pointed out in *Billboard* magazine, 'An opening slot on a major tour doesn't come with a guarantee that the headliner's audience will embrace you.' Luke was all too aware of the difficult balancing act they were expected to perform when he told the *Sun* newspaper, 'We thought [One Direction] were cool, but we did look at them as a pop band and we didn't want to be that.' He clarified this: 'We looked up to the likes of Blink-182 and Green Day, so we felt that it would be kind of weird for us and we didn't know what to do.' Making the differentiation between seeing the type of band you expect to be sharing the stage with One Direction, and the type of band they actually were sharing with was a tough one, but as Ashton noted, it didn't have to be so black and white. 'People get confused because we're young and we have a female fan base. But so did Fall Out Boy. Pete Wentz was the Justin Bieber of 2007. Girls loved him, they obsessed over him.'

Weighing the situation up, those around the boys knew it was too good an opportunity to miss, and a few casual meet-ups with One Direction put the boys' minds at ease. As soon as everyone was in a room together, everything clicked, as Luke confirmed: 'We met the guys and thought they were awesome.' Any criticism that the boys were 'selling out' was swiftly dealt with by Michael, who firmly stated: 'Ask any bar band, "Would you rather go from this to flying first class and staying in nice hotels?" I guarantee every single one of them would say, "Hell yeah!"'

It looked like this was an accurate description of the lives the boys would be leading for some time to come. When the support slot was eventually announced in February 2013, the 5SOS boys had already been away from their families for over two months. During a short break in recording over the Christmas period, only Luke had flown home to Sydney, with Michael staying in London while Ashton joined Calum as he took a trip to Scotland to reconnect with his Scottish heritage. With a 100-plus date tour ahead of them, the boys were contemplating being on the road for almost nine further months, with only a few short breaks to fly home to Australia – they were not going to see much of their friends and families over the next year or so. It would be a huge sacrifice, but the boys all knew that the thing that would help them get through it was the fact they had each other, and the support of their thousands of loyal fans, the 5SOS family.

The decision to go on the tour also meant postponing any serious thoughts of 5 Seconds finishing their album in the foreseeable future. Being on the road and working to such a punishing schedule meant there would be limited opportunities to concentrate on writing and recording the rest of the material they needed to fill it. An option was that they could have polished up the tracks they already had, added a few covers, and released the record while their profile was at a high during the tour, but that was never the album the boys had dreamed of making. They wanted to take their time and make sure every song was something they could be proud of, and more importantly, that they had a hand in creating themselves – 5 Seconds had no intention of quickly recording a bunch of other people's songs. While they respected the work of some of the more traditional pop acts, they didn't necessarily want to be too closely associated with that genre of music or be seen trying to make a fast buck during their moment in the spotlight, or rather, One Direction's spotlight. As Ashton later told *USA Today*, 'We didn't really realize we were a boy band until people started calling us a boy band. I understand and we don't care what people call us, as long as we're making the music we love.' It was this commitment to stick with their own unique sound that had first excited the 1D boys in the first place, and by touring alongside a true boy band, it might just help people understand the difference.

The chance to turn One Direction's audience on to what 5 Seconds were doing was too good to pass up, as they explained on *60 Minutes*: 'By them taking us on tour, it's given us the chance to show their audience a rockier side of pop.' Ashton spoke further about how he and his band mates thought of themselves: 'We're not a boy band – we're a band. We don't want to be called the next One Direction. That's not us.' Luke was keen to point out that joining the 1D tour would not alter their sound, reaffirming their determination to remain true to their roots. 'A lot of bands have to change what they sound like, but we are exactly the band that we want to be: a pop band, definitely, but we've got a rock and punk edge … We're not trying to be anything that we're not. We're not the new anything. We're the first 5 Seconds of Summer.' He continued this theme in the *Sydney Morning Herald*: 'People were already calling us the new One Direction in Australia, but in our minds we're a lot different from them … We play guitars. We're rockier. But we thought that if you put us right next to each other, it would actually show people how different we are.'

While it's true to say the boys had plenty of time to come

to terms with what the rest of 2013 would bring – it seems the idea of the 1D tour had been more or less in the bag for six months, with only the details needing to be ironed out – the reality of heading out to play the impending dates was something else entirely. Calum explained to *Seventeen* magazine, 'I don't think we can really prepare for that. We're pretty scared, but I think we're kind of hiding it at the moment.' Michael was quick to agree: 'None of this has sunk in for us; it's surreal to think we will be on the same bill as a band who are on such a worldwide scale.' He illustrated just how fast everything was moving, saying, 'Now I look at my calendar in my iPhone and it goes from doing our thing, doing our thing, four shows at the O_2 Arena in two days! It's crazy.' Ashton was similarly blown away by the prospect of joining their 1D mentors on the road, telling Ireland's *The Late Late Show*, '[One Direction have] given us the biggest opportunity of our lives, you know? … We're just from my garage in Sydney!'

As the tour's first dates loomed and the boys gathered their thoughts, Calum told Fuse online, 'I guess you can't really rehearse for stadiums. You have to just be thrown into the deep end and go from there. We're really just mentally preparing for what's about to happen.' All too quickly, the build-up was over and the day arrived when the boys were set to play their first show with One Direction.

The scale of the tour was mind-blowing, with the first show taking place at London's O_2 Arena where they would face nearly 20,000 screaming fans. While it's true the majority of those people were there to see One Direction, 5 Seconds of Summer were determined to make a good first impression. Ashton later told the OCC website, 'Our first show with 1D was pretty special … we had to take it from garage playing to arena playing – it was crazy!' Continuing the story in an interview for HMV's website, he said, '[The] first time we played with them we'd done maybe twenty shows, and suddenly we were playing arenas and in front of thousands of people. We literally went from playing to twelve people in pubs to that … I looked up at one point, to see 18,000 people, all of whom seemed to be into it, it was crazy.' Calum confirmed how much of a shock to the system it all was: 'I don't think I moved from one spot that whole show, I was just frozen there.' Michael spoke for the whole band when he said, 'If we'd told ourselves two years ago where we'd be now, we wouldn't have believed it.'

It was a very steep learning curve, but the band were undoubtedly making plenty of new friends as they took to the stage every night in front of thousands of One Direction fans. While never giving less than 100 per cent, the boys were fully aware they might not necessarily be playing for a crowd who understood exactly what 5 Seconds of Summer were about. Ashton underlined that the boys understood they were the support act and that they had a job to do: 'We need to respect that we're here to warm up the crowd for the headliner, [who] has sold out the stadium.' Despite their position on the bill, Luke, Michael, Calum and Ashton let loose, turned up the energy and gave the crowd a show to remember. 5 Seconds of Summer were on a mission to convert the Directioners and invite them to turn coat and join their ever-expanding 5SOS family.

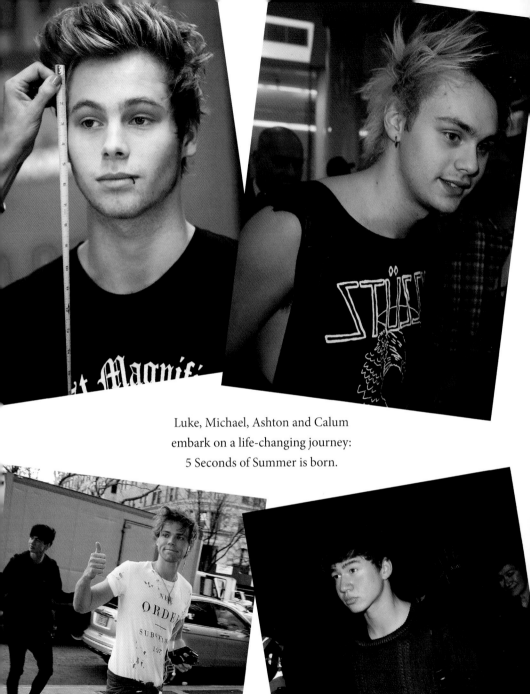

Luke, Michael, Ashton and Calum
embark on a life-changing journey:
5 Seconds of Summer is born.

It didn't take long for them to gain a fanatical following, thanks in part to their heavy presence on social media and close engagement with their fans.

But even the hardest-working boys need some down time. (**Left**) Calum and Ashton have fun at the docks before a gig in June 2013; (**below**) Luke and Calum take a stroll on Sunset Boulevard, LA, January 2014.

(**Above**) (*l–r*) Luke, Michael, Ashton and Calum were thrilled to attend their first BRIT Awards in February 2014.

(**Below**) They quickly get used to the red-carpet treatment as they pose for pictures at the Billboard Music Awards in Las Vegas in May that year.

Doing the media rounds: (**above**) making an appearance on a radio show in Paris, April 2014; (**below**) mingling with the celebs as the boys stand with Kate Hudson at SiriusXM studios in New York.

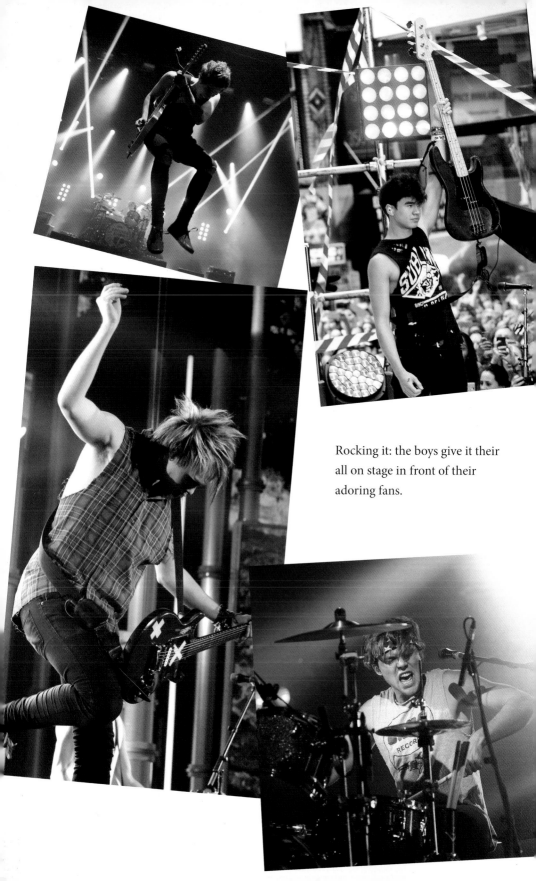

Rocking it: the boys give it their all on stage in front of their adoring fans.

Heroes to their fans,
now superheroes
in real life, as the
foursome take part in
an abseiling stunt on a
London landmark to
promote their self-
titled debut album in
July 2014.

No five-second sensation: the band has had a meteoric rise, and this is only the beginning.

CHAPTER NINE

TAKE US HOME

'How crazy, never in a million years I would've thought I'd be this far from home with our band.'
ASHTON IRWIN (@ASHTON5SOS), TWITTER

The Take Me Home Tour would send 5SOS around the world, and as Calum told *Billboard*, 'Some of those countries we didn't even know existed.' With over 100 shows to perform before the end of October 2013, it promised to be a tough schedule. Tours on such an enormous scale need to run like clockwork – with hundreds of personnel and truckloads of equipment travelling thousands of miles from city to city every few days – and, as such, the boys had a meticulously planned timetable that they were required to follow to the letter. They knew where they needed to be at all times, with rest days and time away from the tour scheduled to the last second. Their typical weekly routine became two or three nights performing, followed by a day off – which was usually spent travelling to the next city or country – and then another two or three consecutive nights on stage. But, despite the enormous physical strain they were being put under, it's safe to say the boys were having the time of their lives, undertaking the shows with renewed enthusiasm on each and every occasion. Thankfully, their efforts were being suitably rewarded, and the reception they received was far from the feared half-hearted cheers and muted applause handed out to some support acts – especially if the main attraction happens to be One Direction.

In an interview with the Alter the Press! website, Luke outlined the spectacle they intended to create with their live show: 'It's going to be really guitar-driven, very high-energy … We like our shows to [have] a big party vibe … We want it to be an amazing experience … We want a show that fans can get involved in.' Determined to prove they deserved their place on the tour, they wanted to give the thousands of 1D supporters a show to remember. With energy levels through the roof, it's little wonder the boys were working up a sweat every night. Ashton related to *AwesomenessTV*, 'I usually cut up a shirt … I don't know why, I kind of like minimal clothing on stage because I get really sweaty. So I just cut something up to make it a lot smaller.' Minimal clothing on stage? Now there was a concept the 20,000-strong audience could really get behind!

It's clear why the response they received was bordering on ecstatic.

Like many rock bands spending days on end travelling from one city to the next, 5 Seconds of Summer began creating their own pre-show routines. However, they fell far short of some of the outrageous or questionable antics of certain out-of-control rock groups. Ashton told Australia's *60 Minutes*, 'We just hang out. It's important that the dressing room is kind of calm.' Calum explained, 'Our pre-show ritual is pretty much listening to a lot of music. It varies from, you know, a bit of Slipknot to a bit of Katy Perry ... depending on how we feel.' Michael was quick to add that, aside from 'listening to heavy metal', the weirdest thing the boys do together was a lot less rock and roll: 'We kind of just brush our teeth.'

As the Take Me Home circus travelled the length and breadth of the UK, the 5SOS boys were keen to treat every night as a lesson in how to grab (and hold) the attention of an arena-sized audience, and eagerly watched and learned from all that was going on around them. They had been handed the unique opportunity to take a look behind the curtain and see how a show of this size was put together, and while it may have dispelled some of the magic involved, they were witnessing first-hand what it takes to deliver such energized levels of performance and stagecraft. At the same time, they were picking up plenty of crucial tips from their considerably more experienced fellow tour mates on how to survive life on the road. It was a completely different lifestyle to anything the boys had previously encountered. They had, of course, toured before, but on a much smaller scale. The distances covered and the relentless forward momentum involved in keeping a tour of this magnitude going was virtually incomprehensible to the 5SOS lads, and the gigs they'd played previously seemed insignificant in comparison.

Fortunately, they were in good hands, and One Direction were always available to offer support and advice. Calum revealed to *Seventeen*, 'Learning how to tour from the lads really changed our lives,' and Ashton was keen to explain to *USA Today* just how much his respect for the 1D boys had grown over the course of those first few weeks: 'Just the way they handle day-to-day life being One Direction, it's a cool thing to watch … The boys work so hard, and I don't think people on the outside really understand how much pressure they're under.' Luke reaffirmed Ashton's point, 'I think we observed how they work and their work ethic … They take it very seriously, but at the same time they have a lot of fun on the road with everything they do.'

There was one barrier to some of the fun, however. 'There aren't too many pranks [on tour] – they have scary security guards. We avoid the security guards as much as we can,' revealed Calum. But they couldn't prevent all of the tricks boys get up to: 'There's usually a lot of fruit throwing, though … [One Direction] are really funny guys. Their humour is really similar to ours.'

Soon the four were beginning to relax, and each new experience helped in transforming the band's approach to live shows, as they told HMV. 'I think it really developed our sound, playing in arenas like that made us such a better live band,' stated Ashton. Michael confessed how much their style had been forced to develop to fill the cavernous arena spaces they were now playing in: 'Even how you move, you have to exaggerate everything you do, so people at the back of these huge rooms can feel the same energy as the people at the front … Usually live, our songs are a bit more bare, stripped back to drums, guitars, bass and vocals.' Luke illustrated how gigs on such a large scale had raised new problems. 'You think about everything: "How can I make this guitar riff or this drum hit sound absolutely huge in an arena?"'

Life on the road can be hard, being away from home and travelling constantly, but the boys were taking strength from one another. Michael affirmed, 'Sometimes when we have a tour bus, it's like our little home. But other than that, we're always around each other. Home is where the band is.' It was tough, but the whole group was enjoying the experience immensely. 'It's the most beautiful thing in the world for a musician to have people looking at you while you are doing what you love the most in the world … It's the best feeling,' Ashton confessed to *60 Minutes*. Calum confirmed his band mate's sentiment, saying, 'The best part is when I look over and I'll see Luke and I'm just, "Wow, I remember you in the music room just jamming on guitar." It's very overwhelming.'

Those shambolic practice sessions and performances to a handful of extra-loyal fans were rapidly becoming a distant memory; 5 Seconds of Summer were morphing into an exciting and seriously polished live act.

The British leg of the tour came to an end in mid-April, when the boys were scheduled to take a well-deserved six-week break. By way of celebration, they planned a small acoustic gig in London. The Barfly show would be a real landmark performance for the band, representing the first time the boys had ever played a headline show outside of Australia and New Zealand. Unsurprisingly, the demand for tickets far outstripped the venue's limited capacity of around 200 people, meaning the show quickly became the hottest ticket in town. With interest in the band so high, they arranged another similar event at the Ruby Lounge in Manchester, which would take place a couple of days after they had played their last gig, for the time being at least, with the 1D boys. Both performances turned out to be an enormous success. After, the boys posted a very special message to their fans – 'Today we played our first ever show outside of Australia! And we just want to say thank you for everyone's support! Today was a special day for us … Love you all!'

The Take Me Home roadshow was set to continue on its route without them, travelling across mainland Europe through May and early June. Another artist, Camryn, had been booked to play the European dates, having been one of the support acts on the Up All Night tour the year before.

These weeks away were a welcome respite from life on the road for Luke, Michael, Calum and Ashton, but it was definitely not something they could consider as time off. Spurred on by the success of these headline shows, the boys announced another solo London gig, this time at the O$_2$ Islington Academy, a much larger venue with a capacity to hold an audience of over 800. The invitation posted on the band's Facebook page read, 'These shows are gonna be totally epic and we cannot wait to hang out, party and go crazy with everyone,' and it proved to be too enticing for the fans to ignore. Yet again, demand far exceeded the availability of tickets and the show sold out in under two minutes. In order to go some way towards meeting that demand, two more shows were added – another at the Islington Academy and a third at Birmingham's O$_2$ Academy 2. Both sold out within minutes.

As well as playing a handful of solo shows, the boys continued to write and record songs for the album. It was during this period that they completed the track 'Try Hard', which Calum and Luke had written alongside Richard Stannard, Seton Daunt, Ash Howes and Tom Fletcher of McFly. The boys even managed to find the time to take a day trip to the seaside town of Blackpool on the north-west coast of England. They intended to film the video for the song on the roller coasters and fairground rides of the famous Pleasure Beach, as well as enjoy the other attractions of one of the UK's most popular amusement parks. The lads posted, 'Was so much fun filming this. The second time we'd ever been to a theme park, we had it shut down for us. CRAZYYYY.' The boys would enjoy the privacy of their very own amusement park for the duration of the filming, spending several hours lip-synching to the track on some of the biggest and fastest roller coaster rides in Britain. A far cry from their homemade videos, it was not the easiest of shoots for some of the boys – Michael looked particularly queasy in some of the fairground scenes!

By the middle of May, with the first thirty-six dates of the One Direction tour, a handful of sold-out UK solo shows and a heap of newly written and recorded songs all under their belts, it was time for Luke, Michael, Calum and Ashton to head back to Australia. They said a fond farewell to their British fans on Facebook, writing, 'We are so lucky to have been so, so welcomed over here in the UK & Ireland by everyone that has discovered us and supported us! You are all such dedicated supporters and we cannot ask for anything more, you are making our dreams come true faster than we could have ever imagined! Thank you. See you soon! Love always and always.'

It was clear to see the effect the extra exposure was having on the band's profile, as the 'Heartbreak Girl' video reached one million views on YouTube and the boys' official Facebook page passed 150,000 'Likes'. Their One Direction gamble had certainly paid off. With renewed confidence and a real sense of pride, the boys were going home, and they couldn't wait to reconnect with their friends and family after such a long time away. There was also something in the pipeline for the boys' most loyal fans. In exchange for the hero's welcome they were no doubt about to receive, the band had a special homecoming gift for the 5SOS family.

CHAPTER TEN

HOMECOMING

*'It's cool to come home. We wouldn't be any-
where without our Sydney fans, or our Australian
fans. Those 12 people who were at the first show
we played – they're the reason we're here now.'*
LUKE HEMMINGS, AUSTRALIAN *DAILY TELEGRAPH*

The boys announced they would be playing a very special
homecoming gig at the Oxford Art Factory in Sydney
on 21 May 2013, shortly after their return to Australia. The
venue held an important place in the boys' hearts, being
one of the first hometown venues they'd played at after
fully committing to the band and taking 5SOS out on the
road. They saw it as a sincere thank you to their first local
supporters – it would undoubtedly be something of a relief
playing to a relatively small crowd of 500 friendly faces,
rather than the tens of thousands of baying fans they had

been facing every night on the One Direction arena tour.

As if the Art Factory show wasn't enough, within hours of touching down, the boys revealed they would be taking to the road in June for a series of Australian headline dates, cheekily going under the name of the Pants Down Tour. They wrote on their Facebook page: 'So excited to finally be home … we missed you guys heaps … and we really want to see as many of you as we can while we are here. So we have some epic news!! We are doing an Australian tour starting next week … It's gonna be bad ass.' Clearly, the boys did not mean to waste a moment of the break from their Take Me Home duties, and they intended to give their Australian fans a sneak peak of what to expect from their set when the 1D tour eventually rolled into their hometowns in a few months' time.

The sold-out Oxford Art Factory gig was a real highlight for the 5SOS lads. Their hardcore Australian fans had waited a long time to see them again – it was almost a full year since their last solo show on their home turf – and the band were determined to prove their patience hadn't been in vain. Ashton was particularly keen to get back on stage and show everyone what they'd been missing, posting a couple of days before the start of the Pants Down tour, 'At home and extremely bored tonight, makes me realize the only thing I'm good at is being on a stage performing for you guys.' The band knew that in this relatively relaxed setting they had the chance to show off some of the new material they had been working so hard to complete, as well as letting everyone see their improved skills as musicians and performers. It would seem no one was disappointed by the performance they gave that night and it proved to be the homecoming the boys had dreamed of during their time away from Sydney.

Eager to keep up the momentum, the boys uploaded 'Try Hard' on 1 June 2013, premiering the video they'd filmed in the UK at the Blackpool Pleasure Beach the previous month. The song and video would become a real fan favourite, having clocked up nearly 13.5 million views on YouTube at the time of writing, and, after a period of being available as a free download, the song was finally officially released as part of the *Don't Stop* EP in 2014.

With only a fortnight to go before they jetted off to rejoin One Direction on the US leg of their Take Me Home tour, the 5SOS boys prepared themselves for their own. This would be another landmark event for them, as they would not only play in the Western state's capital city of Perth for the first time, they would also be playing to their largest headline crowds to date, with each venue on the Pants Down roadshow capable of holding an audience of over 1,000.

The tour was another resounding success for 5 Seconds of Summer. They were greeted at every airport by hundreds of screaming supporters, and each show seemed to be bigger and better than the one before. The boys were determined to let their hair down, and the party vibe they had promised the fans was front and centre at every gig.

As the tour came to an end, the boys had America on their minds. This would be their first trip to the US and they couldn't wait to meet their American followers for the first time. They started a '5SOS vs Food' hashtag on their social media pages and posted, 'Less than a week before we fly out to the USA!!! Sooooo excited. First stop, FLORIDA. What should we do when we arrive? Send us some #5SOSVSFOOD suggestions.' The boys were thinking with their stomachs: 'We want to see photos of all the USA food you think we should be eating on tour and where we can find them – stuff like Philly cheese steaks, hot dogs, Buffalo wings!! Upload them on Tumblr using #5SOSVSFOOD.' Sparking a flood of suggestions and pictures from their followers around the world, the boys certainly wouldn't be stuck for ideas for what to eat on this leg of the tour – they may even forget how much they missed Nando's!

With their menus sorted, Luke, Calum, Michael and Ashton posted, 'Sooo keen to get back on the TMH tour!! USA, see you soon.' They were ready for their next big adventure. 5 Seconds of Summer were about to live their very own American dream.

CHAPTER ELEVEN

AMERICAN DREAM

*'The sky's the limit, I guess. We've already passed
every goal we've ever had.'*
MICHAEL CLIFFORD, AUSTRALIA'S *60 MINUTES*

Every band dreams of making it big in America. As the birthplace of rock and roll in the 1950s, the country claimed its place in music history, and it has maintained its status as one of the most important centres of musical creativity and innovation ever since. From iconic solo artists such as Elvis Presley, Frank Sinatra, Madonna and Michael Jackson to legendary bands like Fleetwood Mac, the Eagles, The Beach Boys and Nirvana, America has been the home of some of the most successful and influential artists in the world. As such, achieving recognition in the US is still considered the pinnacle of success in the international music industry.

Many acts who have achieved great things in their own countries have tried and failed to make it in America. Robbie Williams, arguably the UK's biggest male solo artist, who regularly plays sold-out, arena-sized gigs in Britain and across Europe, while also selling millions of albums in these territories, has struggled to gain any momentum in the US. Similarly, one of the UK's most successful girl groups, Girls Aloud, who managed to score a remarkable run of twenty consecutive Top 10 singles and five multi-platinum albums, also failed to make much of an impression.

The failure to break America by some of the UK's most respected and hard-working artists makes the success of One Direction all the more remarkable. The spread of 1D fever through an army of American Directioners delivered the boys three US Number-One albums in under two years and created sufficient heat to ensure their first world tour in 2012 would go on to generate an estimated $60 million in ticket sales alone. In terms of exposure, with 1D's Take Me Home tour consisting of more than twice as many shows as the last one, the potential rewards for 5 Seconds of Summer were almost beyond comprehension. Making a splash on their US debut performance would not guarantee success, but it was a pretty good base to work from.

Finding an American audience for their brand of guitar-heavy pop-punk would not necessarily be easy. Although US audiences had taken the traditional boy band to their hearts, turning Backstreet Boys, *NSYNC and indeed, One

Direction, into household names, in recent times they had been fairly resistant to bands featuring boys who played their own instruments. 5 Seconds of Summer's UK equivalents, Busted and McFly, had failed to find any lasting success across the Atlantic, and the nearest comparative US acts to strike a chord in their own country were Hanson and the Jonas Brothers. 5 Seconds would just have to get out on stage every night and prove themselves worthy – and it wouldn't be the first time. Buoyed by the rapturous response to their recent Australian solo shows, there was no denying they were more than ready for the challenge.

The first show back on tour, at the BB&T Center in Sunrise, Florida, was certainly a baptism of fire, playing to a sold-out crowd of over 20,000 fans, but the boys whipped up a storm, prompting them to post on Facebook: 'It was AMAZING!!! Had so much fun, thank you.' As they moved on through the Southern states and back up through Washington, Philadelphia and Massachusetts, the boys announced that they planned to play a series of headline acoustic dates, with chances to meet the band afterwards. Alongside their scheduled One Direction support duties, they would play solo sets in several key cities along the tour's planned route. They wrote online, 'WE WANNA DO ACOUSTIC SHOWS everywhere we can whilst on Take Me Home tour over USA. What do you think?' Their first US solo show was due to take place on 17 June at The Studio at Webster Hall in New York, and when tickets went on sale, they sold out within three hours. The answer to the boys' question was strongly in the affirmative.

They arranged further acoustic sets in Boston, Chicago, Los Angeles and an additional show at the Toronto Opera House, their first solo performance in Canada. After each gig, the boys took the time to post hundreds of meet and greet photos to the official 5 Seconds of Summer website and social media pages, as always keeping their new fans as connected to the 5SOS family as possible. To further illustrate just how far and wide the family was growing, the boys' website now featured a map where fans could upload their photos and pinpoint their location using the hashtag #5SOS360. It wasn't long before there were markers covering every corner of the globe.

At the point 'Heartbreak Girl' was close to hitting 3 million views on YouTube and 'Try Hard' was passing its one millionth, the boys played their biggest show to date, rocking out in front of 30,000 fans at the Hersheypark Stadium in Pennsylvania. If this show demonstrated one thing, it was that 5SOS could entertain a massive audience just as well as their headlining tour mates, and were well on their way to becoming as much of a phenomenon, with an army of fans to rival that of the Directioners.

The first leg of the tour, and the boys' subsequent time back home in Australia, had prepared them for anything the American audiences could throw at them – they just didn't expect to have to take that belief quite so literally. As Luke explained to the *Sun* newspaper, 'We've had plastic boobs thrown at us. They are hard to explain … I think I threw them back at the crowd.' Michael added, 'I think we've all got really good at dodging stuff on stage … We get some bras thrown. Ashton once got a Rubik's cube thrown at him – it was like they were asking him to solve it or something.' It would seem that the US fans were holding the boys to their promises that each concert would be a party they would never forget – and they were desperate to get as much attention from the band as possible, even if it meant distracting them from the job at hand with a well-aimed missile.

While the fans' antics were getting pretty bizarre at the concerts, the boys were not experiencing quite the same amount of attention as their 1D companions, with mobbed hotels and room invasions a frequent possibility. But as Michael stated, he was looking forward to a time when they might experience the same type of crazy fan attention. 'We've heard stories from other people about going into their hotel showers and a fan is already in there. But that hasn't happened. I reckon that could be funny, actually.'

As the summer progressed, aside from the scheduled Take Me Home arena shows, the solo acoustic gigs and the accompanying meet and greet events, the boys were also trying to conduct as many local radio interviews as possible – inch by inch, town by town, city by city, 5 Seconds of Summer were spreading their word across America.

The boys managed to use one of their scheduled days off

to visit NASA's Johnson Space Center in Houston, Texas, where they explored the site's collection of space vehicles and memorabilia and were lucky enough to be allowed to meet some former astronauts. They were even granted access to visit the Mission Control Center. Undoubtedly, Calum's inner nerd was experiencing a serious meltdown. Their increasing fame certainly seemed to be opening doors for the lads to new and varied encounters outside of their fledgling careers, which they would never have otherwise had.

As July turned into August, and with the end of the second leg of the tour in sight, the boys started to think about life after their extended stint with One Direction. They still had the Australian leg of the tour to complete in September and October, but after that they were on their own. They announced they would be performing another headline date at the end of November in London, this time at the prestigious venue, KOKO. Yet again, the demand for tickets was enormous, and the show sold out almost instantly. A second date was quickly added, and it too went immediately.

KOKO is a quirky theatre in London's Camden Town. With its relatively small stage area, balconies and private boxes, it has become one of London's most popular music venues, playing host to countless special events, including artist launches, album parties and one-off gigs by huge international stars. With a capacity of just over 2,000, it is the perfect-sized venue to perform big shows in what feels like an intimate environment. Prince performed one of his legendary 'secret gigs' at the venue in 2007, and a couple of years earlier both Madonna and Coldplay caused quite a storm when they decided to use KOKO as the location for the launch events for their new albums, *Confessions on a Dancefloor* and *X&Y*, respectively. For 5SOS, these high-profile performances, with various media types present, would signal the triumphant return of the band to their adopted home in London, and kick-start the next important phase of their career.

As they left the stage of the Staples Center in Los Angeles, California on 10 August 2013, it was time for them to bid farewell to One Direction, for the time being at least, and they posted a message on Facebook, saying, 'The 1D boys have given us a special, amazing and crazy chance to show the world what we can do. We will forever be thankful. We'll make ya proud.' After playing in the shadow of the enormous 1D machine for the best part of a year, it was almost time for 5 Seconds of Summer to break out on their own, but they still had some big steps to take, including signing a record deal and finishing their first album.

For Luke, Michael, Calum and Ashton, the entire Take Me Home tour experience was proving invaluable in terms of exposing the band to legions of potential new fans, as well as turning them into a much more respectable live act – they had clearly become a much tighter unit on stage, and displayed an unrivalled energy and charisma. This, along with the growing maturity in the material they were writing and producing, was setting them apart from virtually every other pop act around. But if the band was to make any real inroads in the international music industry and get the recording of their debut album finished and ready for release, they would need to have the help (and financial clout) of a major record company. Only with major label know-how and a full marketing team behind them could 5SOS hope to get the international launch they had earned. The time had come for 5 Seconds of Summer to finally sign their first proper recording contract. Finding the perfect label to coordinate the release of their debut album, and provide the band with a home for their future output, was one of the final pieces of the puzzle to fall into place. However, before they could commit to any deal, there was one more major decision the boys had to make – and it was a big one.

The two separate strands of the boys' management team had decided to end their business partnership, giving the band the perfect opportunity to re-assess and restructure their management arrangements. In an effort to cause as little disruption as possible and maintain the momentum they'd already started to build, they began looking for a new partner to work alongside elements of their existing set-up. One candidate stood head and shoulders above the rest – Modest! Management. As the management team who had signed One Direction, as well as several other *X Factor* finalists including Olly Murs and Rebecca Ferguson, Modest! were arguably the best equipped to understand the needs of the band and help build their profile internationally. While Modest! might have seemed a straightforward choice, with suitable experience and the resources to take 5 Seconds of Summer where they wanted to go, the decision to sign with them would prove to be a fairly controversial one.

Up until this point, the band had been successfully co-managed by Adam Wilkinson and Matt Emsell's Wonder Management, an arrangement that had allowed the boys to navigate their way through the minefield of the music industry during the earliest stages of their career, book their first tours and helped them cope when they first took to the road with One Direction. Luke's mother, Liz, explained to *60 Minutes*, 'They've had some pretty good grounding so far 'cos the people around them at the moment are like a family. They call them their "tour family", so they really do look out for them and look after them.' Wilkinson and Emsell had been a close-knit team, involving the band in every major creative and business decision, acting more like parents than business associates, and there was no doubt that at every turn they had the boys' best interests at heart. However, Wilkinson had grown increasingly tired of certain elements of the artist management business. He told Music Network, 'I felt quite detached from my passion … I entered the music industry because I had a deep love of music and I was finding more and more with artist management that I was in meetings and travelling more often than being at concerts or in the studio.' Keen to return to a simpler way of life, Wilkinson had made up his mind and amicably gave up his stake in managing 5 Seconds of Summer. Although Wilkinson no longer has any business connections with the band, he still keeps in touch, sure to check up on them whenever they are back in Australia.

Modest! was founded by Richard Griffiths and Harry Magee in 2003. Over the years, the company has nurtured a reputation as one of the best artist management teams in the business, and in 2006 they signed a deal that gave them exclusive rights to sign every contestant who made it through to the live shows of *The X Factor* in the UK. This meant they automatically signed artists such as JLS, Alexandra Burke, Diana Vickers and Cher Lloyd. In time, the company apparently tightened its grip on information regarding its day-to-day running – even now Modest! does not have a Wikipedia page – and fiercely controls media access to its clients.

Several artists apparently began to feel restricted by their Modest! contracts and some, including *X Factor* finalists Rebecca Ferguson and Stacey Solomon, fought costly legal battles in an attempt to free themselves. The Telly Mix blog reported Ferguson had launched a very public attack on her former managers on Twitter in July 2012, where she alleged she was 'so exhausted I couldn't physically walk on my own but was still told I had to work'. She also complained she felt her management team had 'stalked' her on her own Twitter account to keep track of her movements and said, '[These were the] same people that worked me so much I collapsed and had to say stop!!! I need to see my children. You need to give me time off.'

When the 5SOS fans heard rumours of the potential involvement with Modest!, there was a decidedly unfavourable response. While the management group maintains a good reputation in many quarters, continuing to manage the careers of several extremely successful pop artists such as Little Mix, Alison Moyet, Cheryl Cole and of course, One Direction, 5SOS's supporters worried that the bad press generated by several of the company's dropped acts only confirmed them as being controlling and unsympathetic to their artists, and by extension, their followers. For a group that had built up and nurtured an extremely loyal fan base through direct access and interaction, the thought of 5 Seconds of Summer signing with a management company who might try to use their influence to change the band, or limit their contact, was too much for many of the fans to bear.

Online petitions began surfacing on the internet, urging fans to register their disapproval, and some begged the boys not to sign with Modest!. Soon protests began springing up across the band's social media sites, as well as on various fan sites. The 5SOS team were obviously sympathetic to their fans' concerns, and Luke affirmed their importance: 'We listen to what the fans want and listen to what they want us to do. Then [we] respond to that and try and work with that. We try to make everybody happy.'

The band, and their families, were keen to maintain a

degree of control in their careers and eventually worked out a deal that suited everyone. They entrusted Matt Emsell and the Wonder Management team to continue the work they had started a couple of years earlier, while signing a co-management deal with Modest!. The deal ensured Emsell's day-to-day involvement with the band – and his more personal touch – would continue, while Modest! carried the real industry clout that would look after the group's international launch. With the deal struck, it was time for the boys to go record company shopping.

There had been a lot of interest in signing the band after their early successes back in Australia. But 5 Seconds had made the brave and somewhat unexpected decision to 'wait and see', taking the time to fully realize a vision of how they should look and sound before signing a deal that could potentially stifle the boys' creative input and influence how they would be presented to the world. With their determination to remain a guitar band, writing and recording all their own material, the boys were happy to go it alone for as long as they could. With no label involvement in the early stages of building their catalogue of songs, they had successfully avoided having an outsider dictate the most commercial direction for their music to take. It was clear 5 Seconds of Summer were never going to be another 'puppet' boy band – the decision to remain independent and formulate their own identity as a group had been an easy one – but finding someone else within the music business who understood their vision might prove to be considerably more difficult.

Fortunately, the boys found one company who seemed wholly sympathetic to their desire to remain in control of their own destinies. They had decided to put their faith in Capitol Records and their chairman, Steve Barnett. As Ashton told the OCC website, 'There weren't a lot of people that understood the band's vision but Capitol did.' Modest! founder, Richard Griffiths, had already taken Barnett to see 5SOS at one of One Direction's Dublin shows at the start of the tour to gauge his interest, and he had been suitably impressed. 'They were infectious from the minute they walked onstage,' he told *Billboard*. He revealed that it didn't take long to make his decision: 'One and a half minutes into their first song, we said to Richard [Griffiths], "We are in!"'

Previously, as chairman of Columbia Records, Barnett had been a key figure in orchestrating One Direction's launch and subsequent success in the US. After his appointment as chairman and CEO of the Capitol Music Group in 2012, his reputation as an executive who understands his artists' need for creative freedom was confirmed by Capitol signee, Katy Perry, who told the *Hollywood Reporter*, 'He's an incredible boss ... It's nice to have a head in there who knows what they're doing.' While Perry is undoubtedly the most important artist on the label's roster, they also list similarly unconventional Canadian rock band Arcade Fire among their signings. If ever there were a pair of mavericks who personify the need to allow an artist to fully express themselves, it was Katy Perry and Arcade Fire. This was undoubtedly a reassuring thing for 5 Seconds to hear in such a period of big decisions.

As the home of iconic artists such as Frank Sinatra and Nat King Cole in the 1950s, Capitol made its name as one of the most prestigious labels around, but fell on hard times in more recent years. When the label was acquired by Universal Records as part of its deal to buy EMI in 2012, it was decided to return it to its former glory and re-launch it as a standalone imprint for the first time in its seventy-year history. Lucian Grange, Universal Music Group's Chairman, told the *Hollywood Reporter*, 'When we acquired Capitol, we made a commitment – both to the artist community and to the industry – that we would revive this once-great label … I am enormously proud to see what Steve and his team are doing … The building is buzzing.' Everyone involved with managing the band agreed. It was in this environment that Luke, Michael, Calum and Ashton's creativity would be nurtured and hopefully, flourish, and their dream of what they could achieve together would be fully realized.

Key to that artistic freedom was the offer to give the band their own imprint under the larger Capitol umbrella. This was a guarantee that the boys would have final say on all decisions involving 5SOS and any potential future output. With their own label, they would retain control of any developments in the band's sound and image, and if they wanted to, they would eventually be given the opportunity to sign other bands. With their new management team in place and having signed with a record label in November 2013 who were fully on board and in-tune with the vision they had for their own music, the boys were free to concentrate on what they did best.

Such was their determination to make the strongest debut album possible that, despite having stockpiled dozens of tracks while writing and recording in London, the boys insisted they still had a few more to complete before they would have enough of the necessary quality to deliver the album they had always dreamed of making. It was decided that when their duties on the US section of the 1D tour were over, the boys would stay on in Los Angeles and spend another month writing and recording. This time they would be partnered by some of the brightest songwriting talents the US had to offer, and the foursome were going to meet quite a few of their musical heroes, as well as a handful of legends, along the way.

CHAPTER TWELVE

WRITE, RECORD, SLEEP, REPEAT

'It doesn't suck that we're in the "pop" world we are now, but we're going to grow as a band and people are going to perceive us differently.'
MICHAEL CLIFFORD, *ROCK SOUND*

If the 5 Seconds of Summer boys felt they had been put under a lot of pressure before, they were about to get something of a wake-up call. With only a four- or five-week break from live shows after the second leg of the Take Me Home Tour finished in August, there was a lot of work to be done before they were scheduled to leave the US and re-join One Direction in Adelaide, Australia, towards the end of September.

Luke, Michael, Calum and Ashton would be staying on

in LA, in their own rented house, with the sole purpose of writing and recording another batch of new songs to add to the catalogue of original material they had amassed over the last year or so. Luke explained the collaborative process, so successful in the London sessions, which they intended to continue in LA, to the Coup De Main website: 'We usually go to write with other people and we'll go in groups of two, so for instance, me and Michael will go to a songwriting session, and then Calum and Ashton will go to one. We usually come with an idea to write about or the people that we're writing with will have an idea, and then we'll try and build a song from that.'

As far as the subject matter for their writing was concerned, Luke was quick to point out to the *Guardian* that they were still young lads and no matter who they collaborated with, their songs would reflect that. 'We're not going to write about politics. Maybe when we're older. But we write about being social outcasts as well as girls and stuff.' Calum, talking about how things had progressed since their earliest attempts at writing, told HMV, 'When we started work on the album we got put in sessions with some really big writers, before that we'd only really written in our bedrooms and so our songwriting has really moved on in that time.' Commenting on the band's evolving style, he said, 'We really discovered how we wanted the album to sound as we went along. Our sound developed so much more than we thought it would.'

The London sessions had provided the boys with a much

clearer vision of their own musical direction, with time spent working alongside Steve Robson proving particularly invaluable. Credited with discovering the formula for Busted and McFly, which successfully blended the harder-edged, guitar-driven rock with power pop that was so fundamental to the 5 Seconds of Summer sound, Robson had achieved undeniably impressive results. Yet there was no getting away from the fact that, while hugely popular in the UK, these artists had failed to make much of an impression in the US, and things had moved on dramatically in the music business in the decade since the pop-punk boom of the late 1990s and early 2000s. Although guitar-driven pop was slightly out-of-step with what was going on in late 2013, Nick Raphael, president of Capitol Records UK, insisted in an interview with *Music Week*, 'I don't think any genre ever goes away, it merely comes in and out of fashion, like trainers.' Praising the boys for sticking to their guns, he reasoned their affinity for rock music might stem from living in Australia and being shielded from recent fads and fleeting changes in music tastes, suggesting, 'They weren't influenced by what was fashionable and went with what they liked. I think there's a great honesty to that.'

With Capitol's backing, the boys continued their aim to reflect their earliest musical influences in their work, the distinctly American bands Good Charlotte, Fall Out Boy and Green Day, and inject 5 Seconds' new songs with more of an American rock edge, fusing it with a modern pop twist.

Ashton outlined where they were headed, 'You can hear a lot of our influences in there, from the nineties rock and punk we all got into through to new stuff like Imagine Dragons … [As] much as we are a rock band, we want to be a rock band you'll hear on the radio.' Luke summed it up perfectly by saying, 'We want to be a pop-rock band. We want to be part of both sides.' Capitol were keen to help the group fulfil their ambitions for their music, Raphael told *Music Week*. 'We asked the band to list ten successful pop songs that they would have liked to have recorded themselves … We then found the common thread and started approaching people.' Ultimately, one man would be instrumental in helping the boys fully realize their vision. Veteran rock producer John Feldmann was about to make all the boys' dreams come true.

As a hugely influential figure in the LA rock scene in the late eighties, John Feldmann had had a hand in launching the careers of many future legends of American rock music, including Pearl Jam, Korn, Alice in Chains and Rage Against the Machine. After his band Goldfinger split up towards the end of the 1990s, he turned to songwriting and producing. To date, he is credited with co-writing or producing songs that have generated in excess of $34 million for groups such as Good Charlotte, The Used, All Time Low and Panic! at the Disco, as well as giving pop acts such as Hilary Duff, The Veronicas, Mandy Moore and Kelis the benefits of his expertise. Michael, talking to HMV, explained where their paths had first crossed: 'He came to one of our first rehearsals before we went on tour with One Direction. He sat through and watched and at the end he was like, "Yeah, this will work, let's do something." Then one of us said that we loved All Time Low and he whipped out his phone and showed us their number and was like, "I'll call them up."' So, while the 5SOS boys were busy working their way around the world, wowing the crowds on both sides of the Atlantic, Feldmann was pulling in all the favours he could, setting the boys up with some very special writing partners. Over the course of the next few weeks, the boys would meet with some truly big names in the American rock scene, not to mention some of their idols.

The importance of John Feldmann during this stage of the 5 Seconds of Summer story should not be underestimated. Without a doubt, his personality and relaxed approach in the studio, as well as his professionalism and skill as a musician, had a major influence on the boys' output. His contribution was not limited to opening up his extensive contacts list and bringing outside writers to the table, however; it also extended to his day-to-day input into each track. In Feldmann, the boys had found a worthy mentor. Before he came on board, the likes of Steve Robson and the guys from Busted and McFly had already convinced 5SOS they were on the right path musically, but the latter revealed how initially they had struggled to find the right creative team to understand their vision, especially from a commercial perspective. Ashton stated, 'It was very hard to get producers and label people to understand that because guitars aren't in right now, it's such a pop market [at the moment]. But we had to tell them, "Look, we're only good at guitars!'" It was that determination to keep the guitars front and centre on the majority of the new tracks that had prolonged the whole recording process as the band made sure they got it right, but they stuck to their guns and, as Ashton went on to explain, 'We found producers that let us do that.' Michael discussed how the search eventually led them to Feldmann: 'When we started no one was sure what we wanted to sound like other than us, it took us a while to find the right producers … We talked to lots of people and we narrowed it down to the right few.'

It was an introduction from a friend of a friend of Michael's that had brought Feldmann to the fateful meeting in the rehearsal room ahead of the 1D tour, and it all seemed to click into place. Ashton revealed how Feldmann's previous work and his ability to cross genres had been key to their strong bond: 'He's very smart, he knows how to keep his pop mentality, he doesn't try and cram in heavy breakdowns … He's very diverse.'

The partnership proved to be an enduring one, and as Luke noted, 'He doesn't work us hard, but he does put in long hours … He really bonded with us … he's become one of the band's closest friends.' As one of the boys' key collaborators, Feldmann helped set the tone for much of the recording that eventually made up the 5 Seconds of Summer debut album, having a hand in writing or producing eight of the album's twelve tracks, including 'Kiss Me Kiss Me', 'End Up Here' and 'Long Way Home', as well as '18', 'Good Girls', 'Everything I Didn't Say', 'English Love Affair' and the re-recorded 'Beside You'.

The first number to be pulled from Feldmann's little black book was in order to arrange a session with Alex Gaskarth, guitarist and lead singer of US rock-punk band, All Time Low. Like 5 Seconds of Summer, All Time Low had formed while still in high school, getting together in 2003 to perform covers of songs by Blink-182, and signed their first record deal before they had turned eighteen years old. Gaskarth had become the group's most prolific songwriter, sharing writing credits on the music and contributing virtually all of their lyrics. By the time 2009's *Nothing Personal* was released, the band had become firmly established in the US, scoring their first Top 10 album, and with a hectic touring schedule, they began to make waves elsewhere in the world. Their big breakthrough came with 2011's *Dirty Work* and 2012's *Don't Panic*, both of which hit the Top 10 in the US and even managed to break the Australian Top 20.

Gaskarth had agreed to work with the 5 Seconds boys while he was on a break between completing recording on some new tracks for a special edition of the *Don't Panic* album and starting work on the next All Time Low project. Luke, Michael, Calum and Ashton were genuinely honoured to be working with a man whose music had been a key influence on them, having covered his song 'Jasey Rae' in one of their earliest YouTube videos and as part of the *Unplugged* EP. Michael was particularly star-struck, telling Coup De Main, 'I think the day we collaborated with Alex was probably one of the best days of my life. I still think about it … He's one of my biggest idols and it was just so crazy. Now we're all friends with him and he's so supportive of us … I never thought I'd be in this position.' He continued his awe-filled sentiments while talking to Alter the Press!: 'It was just amazing … I just look up to him so much and when we were writing with him, just seeing him there and shaking his hand and him being like, "It's nice to write with you," I was just so happy to be there.' Calum was similarly humbled: 'His writing skills are amazing.' He also related how much of an early inspiration All Time Low and Gaskarth had been to him personally, 'Early All Time Low is really what got me into writing, and it's so cool that you can hear the progression in Alex's songwriting.'

The time with Gaskarth proved to be very productive, and yielded three songs, 'Kiss Me Kiss Me', 'End Up Here' and 'Long Way Home', co-written with Feldmann, all making the final cut on the boys' album. 'Kiss Me Kiss Me' included co-writing credits for Calum and Luke, while 'End Up Here' and 'Long Way Home' came from sessions with Michael and Ashton.

The boys were almost half way through their LA songwriting residency when the next major collaboration coup was unveiled – 5 Seconds of Summer were heading into the studio with two more of their all-time music heroes: Joel and Benji Madden from US rock band Good Charlotte.

This opportunity was especially important for Luke, who told *Teen Vogue*: 'Those nineties bands shaped us ... [Good Charlotte] were the first band I obsessed over. First album and first concert. They were big.' Another rewarding experience, it produced one of the best songs the boys had worked on to date. 'Amnesia', co-written by Joel and Benji, along with Sam Watters and his writing and producing partners, Louis and Michael Biancaniello, eventually became one of the stand-out tracks on the 5 Seconds record. Released as its third official single, it delivered a Top 10 hit in Australia and New Zealand before its UK release in early September gave the band their third straight UK hit single.

At this point, the London studio sessions with Amy Meredith must have seemed like they happened a lifetime ago. Working with several of their musical heroes had filled the boys with even greater enthusiasm for the writing and recording process and they were eager to keep pushing forward. With now almost a full year's worth of new life experiences to draw from, they were more determined than ever to put their own stamp on the tracks they were making, and they were adamant every song should reflect who they were and what they wanted to say. Luke explained to HMV.com, 'All those big writers brought good ideas to the sessions, but you need to be writing about what's going on in your life. It's got to be original ... Retaining our own individuality is still the most important thing.' It was this idea of achieving the correct balance in each track – gratefully accepting guidance from more seasoned writers and blending this into each song with enough of their own personalities and interests – that appealed to the band. 'We learned a lot from those writers,' Ashton confirmed in the same interview, stating that it was the boys' unique perspective on things that made the songs their own. 'You write differently as your experiences change … People don't have our experiences, only you have that, so you need to keep that with you.'

With that in mind, the boys realized that the songs they had been writing over the last year reflected some very different emotions and painted an interesting picture of how the individual members of the group were evolving as young men. Ashton noted, 'We find we write about missing people a lot more now. We've been away for so long.' The boys' library of music was growing, and, while no one was expecting a bunch of sad songs or weepy ballads, it was true they were now maturing as writers, and the album would demonstrate that. Michael revealed, 'There's a lot of variety on there, which we really wanted.' The record was still a way away, but Luke was keen to state that it was all coming together nicely and beginning to take shape. 'We want the first album to have a similar sound, but to be diverse too … it all diverges nicely on the album, we're really happy with it.'

Although the boys seemed to be working around the clock, spending long days and nights locked away in recording studios or with their heads down writing, they did have some opportunity to let their hair down during their time in LA. They were able to stay connected with their fans by hosting several TwitCam events, attended a baseball game and even invited Kent 'Smallzy' Small – the Australian DJ from Nova FM who had been so supportive of the band during their early career – to take a tour of their LA base. During one particularly eventful night, the boys received some particularly unwanted attention. Calum related to *USA Today* how 'Fans found out where we were staying and they sent us two male strippers, which was pretty funny.' He continued, '[They] had flashlights and were shining them through the window. Michael ran up to me and was like, "There are people trying to break into our house!"' Thankfully, nothing else untoward happened. 'They were in cop uniforms. Like, really tight ones … They just ended up walking away.' Surprisingly, that particular experience has yet to appear as the inspiration for one of their songs …

By mid-September, their time in America was over, and the boys flew back to Australia for a couple of weeks of rest before they re-joined the Take Me Home Tour in Adelaide. After such a long time abroad, they all cherished the little time they had to spend with their family and friends, but equally they were keen to say a thank you to the fans. Requesting as many 5SOS hashtags as possible, the boys announced the arrival of their official Instagram, promising to launch it once the #5SOS trend reached 1.5 million. A couple of days later they were up and running – the boys had created yet another opportunity for their followers to feel completely connected to their favourite band.

By the start of October, as the YouTube video for 'Heartbreak Girl' passed 5 million views, the boys were preparing for the next chapter in their incredible journey. The Take Me Home Tour was about to come to an end, and with it the boys were preparing their next move. For the time being at least, their focus was on playing 5SOS headline gigs and putting the next phase of their masterplan into action – it was time for 5 Seconds of Summer to break out on their own, and nothing was going to stop them from taking on the world.

CHAPTER THIRTEEN

TAKING ON THE WORLD

'I just want people to sing our songs at the top of their lungs in cars, malls, bus stops. Anywhere and everywhere.'
ASHTON IRWIN (@ASHTON5SOS), TWITTER

With another month of writing and recording under their belts, and much of the album now in the bag, everyone was feeling excited about the quality of the new songs. Soon they would need to start making some very tough choices: at some point in the near future someone was going to have to make a call on which were good enough to be included on the band's first album, and which not.

The Australian leg of the Take Me Home roadshow saw 5 Seconds of Summer embark on their most extensive tour on their home turf to date. In six weeks they would play multiple shows in all of the country's main cities, including six nights at the 21,000 capacity Allphones Arena in their home town of Sydney. The demand had been so huge for tickets that the tour was forced to circle back on itself, adding four extra dates in Sydney, before finally coming to an end on 30 October 2013 after three more additional shows at the Rod Laver Arena in Melbourne. The end of the 1D journey was inevitably a bittersweet moment for the 5SOS lads. After the Melbourne performance they posted on Facebook, 'It's been amazing,' before uploading a picture of them together with One Direction backstage. The caption read, 'About time we all got a photo together. Gonna miss these lads, see ya soon boys!' But it was equally clear that touring had taken a physical toll on the band when Calum slept through a feature on 5 Seconds of Summer on an early morning Australian TV show, writing the next day, 'Was going to get up early and watch us on *Sunrise* but ended waking up at 3 p.m.'

The tour had been gruelling and would stand as one of the steepest educational experiences the boys were ever likely to have to face. Along the way they had received valuable lessons in musicianship, stagecraft and how to work a huge crowd into a frenzy of excitement. Looking back on a very eventful period in 5 Seconds of Summer's history, Calum told Punktastic just how much the whole experience had changed the band for the better: 'It was an amazing opportunity for us, progressing as a live band and learning as professionals, I guess. It was a massive learning curve for us.' He felt their time with One Direction had also made them stronger as individuals: 'Three of us were still seventeen during the world tour so we had to grow up pretty quick, being away from home for about a year, so it was hard, but at the same time we wouldn't wanna be doing anything else.'

Such a long and trying schedule would have tested the boys' commitment to the band to its limit, but the fact they stayed the course demonstrated they were in it for the long haul, and aided in strengthening the existing bonds they shared with one another. They had not only grown closer as friends, but as musicians, and had discovered exactly what it takes to turn four like-minded individuals into a much more intuitive and creative whole. Suddenly the dream of becoming a proper band to rival those that had inspired them – Green Day, Good Charlotte and Blink-182 – was well within their grasp. They were now a well-oiled machine on stage, and added to their songwriting efforts, would see them evolve into a force to be reckoned with.

The lads rounded out the year with the planned showcase gigs at KOKO in London, and the announcement of a full UK headline tour in the first few months of 2014. As they had now come to expect, all dates sold out in minutes – 2014 was shaping up to be another incredible year in the band's short history.

As each of the boys posted special 5 Seconds of Summer second birthday messages on YouTube and their Facebook page passed the incredible landmark of 1 million 'Likes', they were nominated for Buzzworthy's Fan-Favorite Breakthrough Band of 2013. When news came in on 18 December that they had in fact won the award, the boys were enjoying a well-earned break with their families. With such acclaim after all their hard work, and everything behind the scenes falling neatly into place, it was time to plan phase two of 5 Seconds of Summer's quest for world domination.

2014 was set to start with a bang. The boys posted online, 'Our break in Australia has been so good, feeling ready to rock again!' On 10 January, the lads were on the move again, heading to LA for more writing and recording sessions. With the band now officially signed with Capitol Records, there was soon a flurry of major news announcements to welcome in the new year, the first concerning their personal record label. In typical 5SOS fashion they turned to their fans to help them decide its name, saying, 'One of the reasons we've got to where we are is because we've always worked directly with you amazing people! What you already do to help us is incredible & having this label helps make sure that we can keep working directly with you guys as we (finally LOL) release our first album.' Promising that fans would have the chance to get involved in the label once it was up and running, they stated, 'First task – WE NEED A NAME … we know you're all just as weird as us so it can be as funny or serious as you like.' They added a few suggestions of their own, including Hi or Hey Records, Try Hard Records, Soft Punk Records, Banana Smoothie Records and

Ketchup Records, and then opened it up for fans to tweet their own ideas. As a response to the suggestions they made themselves, Michael tweeted later that same day, 'Why does everyone think we're not serious about this label? WE ARE VERY SERIOUS PEOPLE.' In the end, the lads announced Hi or Hey Records as the best suggestion, telling the fans, 'You all made it trend #1 worldwide last week and we think it's a pretty wicked name too.'

Work in the studio was continuing at an incredible pace, as all too soon the boys would be on the move again. A few days later they were heading to London, and by 2 February they were finally ready to unveil details of their first official worldwide single. When the band had been considering potential lead singles, 'She Looks So Perfect' kept jumping to the top of the pile. 'We wanted something to really explain what the band was all about,' Ashton told the *Today Show*. 'We get the boy band thing and we just wanted to make a rocking pop song and say, "We're 5 Seconds of Summer and we're different."' The song also acted as a bridge between what fans had seen before and what the band wanted to do going forward. 'We haven't released anything since we were about fifteen. The sort of sound, the image and everything has changed. We've grown up a little bit.'

'She Looks So Perfect' had been written by Ashton, Michael and Jake Sinclair during the LA sessions. In hindsight, it seems like an obvious choice for their first international single release, but it wasn't an instant hit with everyone in 5SOS.

Jake Sinclair was not only an established songwriter, he was also an accomplished musician and studio technician, having contributed to songs by some of 5 Seconds of Summer's favourite bands, including Panic! at the Disco and Fall Out Boy. At some point prior to his scheduled writing session with Ashton and Michael, he had found himself in his local American Apparel store, daydreaming as he waited in line to buy several pairs of the store's branded underwear. He said he noticed the in-store ads, which featured images of girls wearing the underpants, confessing to *Billboard*, 'The brain is a weird place … I just thought, "Oh, it'd be cool if my girlfriend wore these."' He made a quick mental note and went about his business. Flash-forward to his meeting with Ashton and Michael and the idea seemed to fit with something the boys had been working on. 'He showed us it and said, "This is what I've got, this is the idea,"' Ashton revealed to Sugarscape.com. 'We thought it was really cute and sort of expanded on it.' Ashton and Michael completed the session with Sinclair, but soon doubts about the song started to creep into their minds, as Ashton later explained to KIIS 1065 Radio. 'Michael hated it. We wrote it in a day and when we left the writing session, Michael said, "Man, that song sucked." So I was like, "Nah, man, it's a good song." So we pushed through and recorded it.'

The song was an undeniably bold statement. With its opening 'Hey, Hey' chant giving way to a thundering mass of bass and drums, this was clearly no ordinary pop single, and was a double shock to the system for anyone expecting a typical boy band song. The massive chorus soared over some heavy guitars, delivering the kind of instantly catchy hook that ensures the song stays in your head long after the first listen. Played alongside the big hits of the moment – the likes of Pharrell's 'Happy', Beyoncé's 'Drunk In Love' and Lorde's 'Royals' – it was unlike anything else on the radio in early 2014.

The boys announced on 4 February that the download would be available to pre-order via iTunes and the CD single through their website and other online retailers. As the song's release was staggered in different countries around the world, it was made available to order over the course of a few days, and proved to be an instant hit as soon as the respective pre-order went live. Amazingly, the song hit Number One on pre-sales alone in several charts, days before any of the fans had the chance to hear the full version. On 7 February, after posting teaser clips and artwork, the lyric video was uploaded and premiered on Vevo. The fans' responses were almost universally positive, ranging from the simple, 'Was even more perfect than I thought,' to the downright bizarre, 'I burnt my bacon watching the video.' As the initial excitement of the week's events started to die down, the boys posted on Facebook, 'The past week has been crazy. We feel incredibly blessed and grateful.'

The tongue-in-cheek video, directed by Frank Borin, features a diverse group of everyday people – including an

American cop, supermarket shoppers and customers in a diner – who start stripping off their clothes as the song sends them into an uncontrollable frenzy of dancing and lust. Ashton confessed to PopCrush, 'I think we've never wanted anything more than for people to get nude in a video of ours.' He also outlined how the concept developed: 'The director, Frank Borin, came to us with the idea and we're like, "That's absolutely perfect." He's like, "Yeah, the song should put people in a craze and make them want to take their clothes off." And I was like, "Sounds good."' Wary of censorship issues and a possible ban from certain video channels, not everyone in the video ended up in their 'American Apparel underwear', as director Borin explained to *Billboard*: 'American Apparel isn't for every body type … On some people it was too small, or too risqué.' The video ends before the boys remove their own trousers, fearing a shot of them in their underwear would be 'inappropriate', but as Michael revealed, 'There is an edit out there somewhere of us! But it looks really weird … it's like "What do we do now?"'

With everyone suitably covered up, the full official music video for 'She Looks So Perfect' was an instant smash when it premiered on Vevo on the 24 February, and has since gone on to achieve more than 65 million views on YouTube.

Unfortunately, they had very little time to reflect on recent events: they were back in the studio recording the song 'Lost Boy', which Calum and Luke had written with Scouting for Girls front man, Roy Stride. Eager to drum up even more excitement about 'She Looks So Perfect' before its official release in Britain at the end of March, the boys announced a short UK Radio Tour, which would take them to eight major cities around the country, giving press and radio interviews as well as meeting as many new fans as they could along the way.

With their single on the radio, the video playing everywhere and the process of choosing songs for their debut album well under way, 5 Seconds finally felt they had arrived. They now had something concrete to show for all the hard work they had been putting in over the last couple of years, and the decision to take their time, learn how to be a proper band and make the kind of music they felt passionate about was beginning to pay off. Each of the boys had sacrificed a lot to get to this point – having dropped out of school, spent months away from their family and friends and poured everything they had to give into the band. In just a little over two years they had come such a long way. Michael expressed his disbelief to Music Feeds, saying, 'We really never intended to be known worldwide. We just thought a few of our friends would watch the videos, maybe their friends at best.' If heading out on the road with One Direction had proved to be the ultimate education for the band, releasing their own music was definitely their graduation. Now, with their own sound and their own songs, they felt they had waited long enough, and were more determined than ever to kick on. Ashton explained, 'We wanted to stay under the radar for as long as we could … now is the time for us to really show the world what we're about.'

When 'She Looks So Perfect' was finally released in Australia on 23 February, it entered the national ARIA chart at Number Three, before climbing to Number One on its fifth week in the chart. In the UK, however, it was a much more instant success. Released a month later, on 23 March, the song went straight to the Number One spot of the Official Singles Chart, becoming only the fourth Australian artist to hit Number One in the UK, and the first to do so in fourteen years. In an interview with the *Today Show*, Luke recalled the moment they heard they were Number One: 'I remember running into Ashton's room and I was like, "We're Number One!"' The drummer himself exclaimed, 'It was like Christmas. That was exactly what it was like.'

In America, 'She Looks So Perfect' was released at the beginning of April as part of an EP and was thus considered to be an album, rather than a single, making it eligible for their album chart. The *She Looks So Perfect* EP sold a staggering 143,000 copies in its first week on sale in the US and stormed into the chart at Number Two. It was only prevented from attaining the Number One spot by the all-conquering soundtrack to Disney's *Frozen* – an album that had, at that point, sold nearly 2 million records and was enjoying its ninth week at the top of the *Billboard* 200 Album Chart. As a standalone track, 'She Looks So Perfect' eventually peaked at number twenty-four on the *Billboard* Hot 100 singles chart, making it the boys' first US Top 40 single.

As a calling card, 'She Looks So Perfect' had certainly done its job. While the band were hardly unknown in the US, the song's success pushed them firmly on to the radar of the mainstream press and media, who were falling over themselves to interview the lads and tell their story. Thrust into a much brighter spotlight, they were reaching a much wider audience than ever before – the Directioners who had come on board in the last year or so having no doubt helped – and were converting thousands of their own new fans every day.

An unusual side effect of the song's popularity following its release was the reported sales increase in American Apparel underwear. It would seem the brand was now engaging a completely different market, with American Apparel store worker Amber Joyner telling *Billboard*, 'It's more younger types, who would listen to kids' music like that, who weren't very familiar with our brand before.' Iris Alonzo, an American Apparel spokeswoman, admitted, 'I have no idea if it's attributed to the 5 Seconds of Summer song, but there was a 10 per cent increase in US sales of our men's underwear outside of the typical seasonal increase we see in this style in the spring.' Whether or not the upswing in sales could be directly attributed to the shout-out from the boys, Luke told *Billboard* that, so far, the band had not received a parcel of free underwear from the retailer. 'No one from the company has even sent us an email … They're playing hard to get.' Michael told the Coup De Main website, 'I don't think they like us. I think they're annoyed at us.'

The boys felt they had now written all the music they needed for the album, and, as Ashton related to Alter the Press!, there was plenty to choose from: 'We've got [close to] 100 songs written.' There were, however, still a few loose ends to tie up in terms of getting them recorded and finalized. While modern recording techniques meant this could be done while the band was on the move, the boys still had a lot of hours to put in before the album could be considered in the can. In an interview with HMV, Ashton confirmed, 'We've been out in the middle of nowhere just outside Oxford finishing off our album.' Michael explained that they were under quite a bit of pressure to complete their work: 'We were told that time is so short that we needed to cram in recording six songs into two days. Long days.' Calum showed his usual laid-back approach to the strain, joking, 'You could tell we were short on time, the FIFA time fell dramatically.'

With most of the hard work done, and while the finishing touches to the album were being made by the studio, it seemed only logical to spend the rest of this period on the road, playing live and doing as much promotional work as possible. Just days before they started the UK headline tour, which they'd announced at the end of 2013, the boys unveiled further details of their plans for the next few months. With little more than a pause for breath, the boys announced a busy touring schedule that would have them on the road until early May, playing headline shows across Europe, the US and Australia.

First up would be the 5 Countries 5 Days Tour, which would see the band playing shows in five different European countries in just five days, taking in Sweden, Germany, France, Italy and Spain. The week after they would kick off their first US headlining tour in San Francisco, the Stars, Stripes and Maple Syrup Tour, visiting a further nine major cities in North America and Canada. As soon as these dates were completed, the boys were then set to return to Australia for the There's No Place Like Home Tour, which featured dates in Adelaide, Melbourne, Sydney, Brisbane and Perth.

The UK tour was barely underway when, on 5 March, the boys revealed they had some even bigger news for their international fans – they would also be joining One Direction on their next world tour – the Where We Are Tour – as it travelled around the UK, Ireland, Europe and America between May and October 2014. Considering the boys had an album to finish, release and promote, on top of their touring duties, 2014 was proving to be their busiest year yet.

CHAPTER FOURTEEN

WHERE WE ARE

'We want to really make a mark and help people realize that bands are still coming through. I think if people don't give bands like us a chance, they're stopping rock music from growing and progressing and letting new audiences in.'

ASHTON IRWIN, *ROCK SOUND*

At the beginning of May 2014, with less than two weeks to go before they were set to re-join their One Direction buddies and kick-start the Where We Are Tour in Ireland, 5 Seconds of Summer were nearing the end of their No Place Like Home tour in Australia. A couple of weeks earlier, they had played their biggest headline show to date, at the Dome in Oakland, Connecticut, to almost 5,000 fans, and had recently watched their already impressive social media stats continue ever upwards as they passed the 2 million 'Likes' landmark on Facebook.

As 2014 rolled on, the band's popularity was reaching new heights and their status as the 'next big thing' was all but assured. Ahead of the 1D tour, the boys had been putting the finishing touches to their album, with their vast collection of recorded songs having to be painstakingly cut down to a manageable few worthy of being considered for the final track listing. Calum told Fuse Online, 'We're pretty much finished with the album. We've written over one hundred songs now and we've finally whittled it down to twenty or twenty-five.' He added, 'We're really proud of it because we've been writing for so long, so it's good to finally have a body of work of ours.' From the boys' huge stockpile, one song stood out almost as much as 'She Looks So Perfect'.

'Don't Stop' had become a firm favourite, and as soon as it was recorded it became an obvious contender to be released as a second 'set-up' single ahead of the album. The song was written by Luke and Calum during their sessions with Steve Robson, and featured contributions from Michael Busbee, also known as busbee. As a songwriter and producer, busbee had made the same transition as Robson, moving neatly from working in Nashville with the likes of Rascal Flatts and Lady Antebellum to co-writing big pop hits for Alexandra Burke ('Bad Boys'), Timbaland ('If We Ever Meet Again'), Pink ('Try') and Kelly Clarkson ('Dark Side'), among others. His understanding of pop hooks and guitar-based productions made him a perfect fit for the emerging 5 Seconds of Summer sound. Starting with a clatter of drums, chugging guitar chords and an even heavier, slicing riff, it's a good deal more straightforward – and a more punk affair – than 'She Looks So Perfect'. But like its predecessor, it piles on the hooks and, if anything, the chorus is even more catchy than the boys' debut. With a running time of under three minutes, it's a short, sharp, shock of bright and breezy harmonies and boundless energy.

Once the band announced 'Don't Stop' as their next international single – excluding the US where a different track, 'Good Girls', was issued as an album preview song – they promptly uploaded a lyric video to YouTube. It's a very clear indication of just how fast their fan base was growing when even an initial lyric video managed to reach 1 million views in forty-eight hours. What's even more extraordinary is that only a couple of weeks later, when they uploaded the official music video, it achieved more than twice that number of views during the same time period. Ashton took to Twitter to proclaim his disbelief, saying, 'OMG, "Don't Stop" has 2M views, what the hell, when did that happen!'

The lyric video saw the boys fulfil a classically boyish fantasy of becoming superheroes and allowed them to feature as comic-book alter egos. The promo video's director, Sophia Ray, told MTV, 'We thought it was quite a nice, positive touch going down the superhero route.' She confirmed the boys had picked their own superhero names – Luke became

Dr Fluke, Ashton was now Smash, Calum adopted the name Cal-Pal and Michael was transformed into Mike-Ro-Wave. The lads later revealed their hero alter-ego origins in a very funny 'Lost Tapes' video, with Calum admitting he has no real powers, making him 'the worst superhero ever', and Ashton explaining his abilities originated when he was crushed under a pile of gym equipment. Luke is typically reluctant to share too much, but admits his main strength is the fact he has cool gloves and Michael reveals his hero's mantra is 'What you are is what you eat.' Aside from the humour and the boys' patent wish-fulfilment, the lyric video had a more serious message, which saw the band promoting an anti-bullying campaign that had arisen following reports that Ashton's sister had been the victim of bullying at her school. In the lyric video, the boys work together to rescue a red-headed girl from a gang of thugs, and as Ray explained, 'She was inspired by the fan base that the guys have. We wanted her to signify all of their fans – all the people that they're serving through the anti-bullying campaign.'

The official live action video, which came a few weeks later, was directed by Isaac Rentz, who explained the concept in the video's behind the scenes clips: 'The second I saw how charismatic and fun-loving they are, I just thought, "I've gotta use this idea for this band right now."' Shooting the video was an extremely fun experience, Luke telling the *Daily Star*, 'To be honest, we shot so much in those two days making our vid, we could've made a feature film out of it already.'

He sparked rumours they might be following their mentors, One Direction, onto the big screen by saying, 'We'd love to make a film.' While it's not quite a movie, the full video offers a playful insight into the boys' superhero lifestyles and has some very fun moments, with them finding out that work as a superhero is not always plain sailing or filled with much thanks from their rescued victims. Individually, they have varying degrees of success as they save lost cats, help old ladies across the road and confront a scary gang spraying graffiti. It's only when they combine their efforts – as the 5SOS version of the Avengers – that they realize they are stronger and more powerful as a team. A neat reference to the real-life 5 Seconds of Summer origin story, perhaps. Michael admitted, 'I would've happily spent every day in those suits, except when you need to pee, that's really hard.' Ashton had the last word on the whole experience during the behind the scenes video, stating cheekily, 'Being a superhero is pretty awesome. Better than I expected. Tight underwear … I feel good … supported.'

Ahead of 'Don't Stop's' release the boys were scheduled to make their US TV debut on 18 May 2014, after being invited to perform at the annual *Billboard* Music Awards at the MGM Grand Hotel in Las Vegas. Taking the stage at this prestigious music industry event was an invaluable piece of mass exposure, and the decision was made to strategically announce the release of their long-awaited debut album in the run-up to the awards. After a teasing message on the band's social media pages the week before, saying, 'Listening to the album and thinking how proud I am of the lads,' the announcement came on 13 May. The band simply stated on Facebook: 'After three years, we finally get to tell you that … WE HAVE AN ALBUM!!!' They added, 'We've been working on this so hard for you and it feels so good that we finally get to release it. We really hope you'll like it.'

It had been a long process, and the boys had stuck to their guns in terms of making exactly the album they'd wanted to. Ashton explained to musictakeabow.com, 'We took a lot of time being musicians … we really wanted to make it musically awesome … We pride ourselves on making sounds we can be proud of.' When it came to naming their debut, it seemed the band had completely used up all of their creative juices. Luke mused, 'It's a difficult one. We come up with the names for our tours really quickly, it needs to be spontaneous.' The album would end up being self-titled, with the words '5 Seconds of Summer' as the only text on the cover.

The record was due to follow a complicated staggered release strategy, which took into account different countries' release date patterns – some release on Fridays, while others release on Mondays; in the US new albums usually appear on a Tuesday – as well as trying to factor in where the boys would be on the One Direction tour for their availability to promote the album. Thus in Australia, New Zealand and much of Europe the album was due on 27 June, with the UK release scheduled for three days later. Japan would get it on

16 July, while in the US, Canada and Mexico, 22 July would be the launch date. The huge publicity drive surrounding the *Billboard* appearance acted as the perfect platform to start a buzz around the record, and pretty soon, no one could forget it was on its way.

Being handed the opportunity to perform at the *Billboard* Awards was not something the boys took lightly, and as they headed to Las Vegas to rehearse for the show they began to realize just how much it meant to them, and what a massive milestone in their career it really was. For a relatively unknown band, making their television debut in such revered company, they might have been expected to crumble under the pressure. Of course, they managed to keep their cool, which is more than can be said for Kendall Jenner, the reality TV star famous for her appearances on *Keeping Up with the Kardashians*, who was chosen to deliver the boys' on-stage introduction.

Starting off with a brief summary of the 5 Seconds success story, it all went horribly wrong when Kendall, reading from the autocue, started to introduce the band as One Direction. Inexcusable in the eyes of the 5SOS family, but perhaps understandable considering Kendall was rumoured to have been dating 1D's Harry Styles. With their relationship now over, perhaps she had had other things on her mind. After a brief video introduction to the band, the live feed cut back to Kendall as she said, 'They're only getting bigger! Take a look.' Unfortunately, few were able to hear her words as 5 Seconds of Summer had already started their performance.

Sharing the bill with some of the biggest names in music, including Miley Cyrus, Robin Thicke, Jennifer Lopez, John Legend and a holographic Michael Jackson, the boys performed a blistering, energetic version of 'She Looks So Perfect'. *Billboard* reporter Chris Payne called it a 'killer performance', stating, 'Although it was one of the lesser-known songs performed at the show, "She Looks So Perfect's" infectious chorus made it a slick crowd-pleaser.'

It was a triumphant first live US TV appearance and one they would never forget. It also proved to be incredibly important, exposing the band to an even wider and more mainstream audience. 5 Seconds of Summer was the most talked about Twitter account following the performance, with the band's name trending worldwide, and mentioned almost half a million times during the show. While these are impressive social media stats, even for 5SOS, they are all the more surprising because this figure is greater than every online shout-out generated by all the night's other performers added together.

With another key moment behind them, the boys refocused on the build-up to the publication of their debut album. With its position as the last official single ahead of the record, 'Don't Stop' was released in the middle of June, where it peaked at Number Three in Australia and Number One in New Zealand. A couple of weeks later the boys pulled out all the stops to try to secure their second UK Number

One single, with Luke admitting to the *Daily Star*, 'I hope for another Number One but we don't want to get too excited. Number One never gets boring, it's such a big thing. I still wake up thinking about the first one, I don't know what I would do if it happened again.' Joining forces with high-street music retailer HMV for a series of in-store signings during the single's first week of release, the boys even signed 1,000 extra copies of the CD and had them shipped to one of the chain's London stores, only revealing to fans where they were at the end of the week on Twitter. The store reported that 800 of these signed copies had sold within an hour of their location being revealed. The boys' main competition was from former *X Factor* contestant, Ella Henderson, who had finished in sixth place during the 2012 season of the show, and was finally releasing her debut single, 'Ghost', a track co-written by OneRepublic's Ryan Tedder. Michael was closely following the song's chart battle during their first few days on sale and tweeted early in the week, 'Can't even believe "Don't Stop" could actually be in the top three in the UK, so crazy … You guys are epic.' He later added, 'We're really close to getting our 2nd #1 in the UK and it's all thanks to you guys for supporting us.' Sadly, Michael's rallying cry wasn't quite enough, and after a close-fought battle that had seen 5 Seconds of Summer at Number One at the mid-week point, 'Don't Stop' entered the UK singles chart at Number Two, having sold close to 82,000 copies, a mere 3,000 less than 'Ghost'. Calum was gracious in defeat and tweeted, 'I just wanna thank you guys for getting us to number 2 on the UK charts! You are the best! Don't forget it! Thank you, thank you.'

In the US, 'Don't Stop' was not officially released as a single, but was made available as a download, selling 91,000 copies in one week when it was offered to anyone pre-ordering the 5 Seconds of Summer album on iTunes – a figure that was eclipsed by the first-week total of 121,000 downloads achieved by 'Good Girls' when it was made available a few weeks later.

Things were certainly moving in the right direction for 5 Seconds of Summer, and initial reactions towards their new songs from the established fan base were universally positive. New supporters were finding their way into the 5SOS family in rapidly increasing numbers, Ashton celebrating passing the 2 million followers milestone on Twitter by saying, 'Wow, thanks guys, that's freakin' epic! I love ya. You guys grow with us, every step of the way.'

As the band took up their positions alongside One Direction for their first show of the Where We Are Tour in May, it was a chance to also look back and reflect as they noted it was two years since they posted the original 'Gotta Get Out' video. They had undoubtedly come a long way, and had plenty more to commemorate, with Calum posting on Twitter, '4 kids from western Sydney just played a stadium! So proud of the lads, they did so well!'

The one negative aspect of the band's move into the

mainstream was the reaction by some of the longer-serving fans to recent converts to the 5SOS family. As with many groups that start out small and build a devoted and extremely loyal core fan base, the move towards mass acceptance can prove troublesome. For some of the early supporters, the thought of others muscling-in on the thing they considered exclusive, or the threat of losing the close relationship they felt they shared with their favourite band can be too much to cope with. With online message boards and fan sites filling up with arguments about who had been a fan the longest and others expressing their beliefs that people who discovered the band through One Direction were not 'true fans', the boys decided to step in, hoping to defuse the situation and restore harmony in the 5SOS family. Michael used his Twitter account to say, 'People who supported our band from the beginning are the reason we're in the position we are now,' and asked, 'What's with this whole "fake fan" thing?' He went on to say, 'A fan is a fan regardless of what they do, don't judge … If someone likes a band, don't think you're better than them if you've liked them longer, you all discovered that band at one stage #nohate.' While it didn't cut out the problem completely, Michael's comments did seem to deliver the boys' message loud and clear.

5 Seconds' second stint as concert openers for One Direction was certainly going a long way to cementing their reputation as a fun pop band, and was winning them even more young female fans along the way, but the release of

their latest batch of self-written songs was also making other, more serious elements of the music industry sit up and take notice. This unlikely combination of pop fandom and musical credibility saw the band nominated for Best International Newcomer at the *Kerrang!* Awards, only a matter of weeks after winning Fave New Talent at *Nickelodeon*'s Kids' Choice Awards. The unusual position the group found themselves in was best highlighted in alternative music website Alter the Press!'s review for the *She Looks So Perfect* EP. It starts by stating, for the record, that 5 Seconds of Summer are not a boy band. Asserting they play their own instruments and suggesting they shouldn't be judged by who they have opened for in the past, it affirmed, 'This is not the next step in the boy band resurrection; this is 5 Seconds of Summer, the *She Looks So Perfect* EP is their introduction, and it's a pretty damn good one.' It went on to say, 'These boys have so much coming into their own to do, what with this being their starting point, they are bound to be something great.' The review concluded, 'This isn't the next act of the boy band era, but rather the start of a new wave of pop/rock – a wave that was desperately needed in a genre that has been feeling a little stale.'

During the months that followed, it was managing this uneasy balance between beckoning pop superstardom and their wish to be recognized as credible musicians that would become one of the band's greatest achievements.

While it's clear that it was going to take a while to convert the majority of rock fans, understandably suspicious of the more polished and poppy elements of 5 Seconds of Summer's music (as well as their association with One Direction), some elements of the serious rock press were more inclined to accept the band as one of their own. Before long, the boys' obvious commitment to promoting guitar-driven music, their enthusiasm for name-checking the likes of Green Day and Blink-182 as their biggest influences and the long list of impressive writing partners who had worked on the 5 Seconds debut album prompted a U-turn among some of their harshest critics – it was hard to argue with the rock credentials of many of the people the band were involved with, after all. Ongoing working relationships with the likes of All Time Low's Alex Gaskarth, Good Charlotte's Benji and Joel Madden and esteemed rock producer John Feldmann soon saw them welcomed by many of the genre's more open-minded publications. Appreciating that appeasing the ever-growing 5SOS family would also do no harm to their sales figures, articles and interviews started to appear in the likes of *Alternative Press* and *Rock Sounds*, with the latter taking the bold step of not only putting the band on the front of the magazine, but producing four different cover versions, each featuring an individual photo of one of the boys to promote their exclusive 5 Seconds of Summer feature. Even *Kerrang!*, the long-running and self-proclaimed 'Bible' for all things rock, started writing about the band with respect.

When *Kerrang!* revealed the nominations for their annual

awards ceremony, a few eyebrows were raised when 5 Seconds of Summer were included alongside considerably heavier rock acts Crossfaith, Issues, We Came as Romans and State Champs in the Best International Newcomer category. Unfortunately, the ongoing struggle they faced for full acceptance was highlighted when, at the London ceremony on 13 June, they were greeted with a chorus of boos from the audience when they were announced as the winners of the award. The boys took the negative response to their win in their stride, simply stating they were 'Honoured to win the *Kerrang!* Award for Best International Newcomer,' adding, 'Thank you all for voting. You're amazing. Love U guys.' As always, the boys were well aware that it was their real fans that mattered, and they would always be grateful for their support.

The magazine's editor, James McMahon, had freely expressed his feelings about the band previously on his personal Twitter account, saying he thought they were 'rubbish'. Following numerous online attacks from the band's fans, he decided to clarify his sentiments. He took to Twitter again to state, for the record, that his previous comments were largely due to his own personal tastes: 'I did tweet saying that 5 Seconds of Summer are rubbish. Because, y'know, I'm a 33-year-old man with a beard.' He went on to voice his opinion, this time as the editor of the country's leading rock magazine, saying, 'If they help somebody get into [real rock bands] one day, then awesome.'

It is this point that was more eloquently expressed in an article written by Matt Crane and published in *Alternative Press* magazine. Crane was keen to point out that 5 Seconds of Summer's breakthrough was not just a triumph of a major record company successfully marketing a new pop band, but something that also needed to be celebrated within the broader, more serious sections of the music industry. He wrote, 'The band are branded as pop-punk, which they are, albeit the poppiest, most radio-friendly form. In a broader view, what this means is that the massive major-label infrastructure pushing this band is highlighting the fact that they're pop-punk – not trying to change them into a boy band – at a time when pop-punk couldn't be more maligned as a genre by mainstream music culture.' Crane went on to predict 5 Seconds of Summer's popularity could lead to another glut of similarly guitar-driven pop acts, stating, 'The last time we saw an explosion of the genre with the full backing of the music industry, we got Blink-182, Sum 41, Good Charlotte, New Found Glory and more.'

The side effect of each of the 5SOS lads enthusiastically citing these bands as their main influences, as well as name-checking countless other modern rock bands such as Paramore, All Time Low, Mayday Parade and A Day To Remember as their current favourites, Crane speculated, may inspire their fans to investigate further on their own, leading them to a much broader spectrum of guitar-driven rock and metal music. Opening up the floodgates to a brand-new fan base could only be a positive move for any genre of music – with increased interest would come greater investment from record companies, as well as a much-needed boost for smaller music venues and interest across the mainstream media in general. If a dozen other struggling pop-punk bands, who might be in the same position as 5 Seconds of Summer were a couple of years earlier, receive a leg-up from the band's acceptance into the mainstream, creating a mini-movement of guitar-led pop bands, then it could only be a positive thing.

It was into this atmosphere of optimism that the 5 Seconds of Summer debut album was eventually released some weeks later, and while it would not be heralded as 'the saviour of rock music', it was accepted by most elements of the more established 'serious' music press, receiving a fair hearing from the likes of *Rolling Stone, Billboard* and *Alternative Press*, as well as the predicted rave reviews in many of the pop and teen magazines.

As the Where We Are Tour finished travelling around the UK with three nights at the O_2 in London, there was a rare opportunity for the band to spend time with their families. Australia's *60 Minutes* programme decided to bring their mothers over to spend a couple of days in London, and filmed them reuniting with their sons. It was an emotional few days for everyone. It highlighted the fact that over the last year or so, the boys had been away much more than they had been at home, and it was obviously sometimes difficult to cope with the separation. Luke's mother, Liz, told *60 Minutes* how she felt seeing her son on stage in London: 'Just immense pride, amazing pride. It makes me tear up every time … I've seen hundreds of shows … it doesn't matter if it's a tiny venue or Wembley Stadium, I get the same feeling of pride and think, "Wow, that's my baby up there."'

While it was a very welcome break for the boys – they had five days off before rejoining the One Direction lads in Sweden – there was still plenty of work to do. They were still recording possible bonus tracks in a London studio and they were due to make their UK television debut on Channel 4's *Sunday Brunch*. On the show, they were expected to help with a couple of cooking segments, where the boys' culinary skills were put to the test and shown to be sadly lacking, as well as talk about their music, the album and the One Direction tour dates. They finished their appearance by performing a blistering acoustic version of 'Don't Stop' live in the studio.

The boys jetted off to re-join their 1D tour mates as they visited Sweden, Copenhagen and France, with a part of the tour interrupted by a quick jaunt back to the UK to play at Capital FM's Summertime Ball. It was less than a couple of weeks since the boys had played at Wembley Stadium with One Direction, but this time they shared the stage with a host of UK and international pop acts, including Pharrell Williams, Ed Sheeran, David Guetta, Ellie Goulding, Calvin Harris, Sam Smith, Little Mix and Iggy Azalea. The boys played three tracks to an ecstatic crowd, including several

5SOS super-fans with homemade banners and signs. Their set included their own songs 'Don't Stop' and 'She Looks So Perfect', as well as their rocking cover of Katy Perry's 'Teenage Dream'.

The last few days in June saw the boys complete the rest of the European leg of the Where We Are Tour as they passed through the Netherlands, Italy, Germany, Switzerland, Spain and Portugal, but the main draw for the whole 5SOS family was the release of their much-anticipated debut album. It had been a long time coming, but soon a host of new people around the world would fall under the spell of 5 Seconds of Summer.

CHAPTER FIFTEEN

TRACK BY TRACK

'The album? Oh, it's totally finished … Nearly!'
ASHTON IRWIN, MUSICTAKEABOW.COM

The 5 Seconds of Summer debut album is remarkable for many reasons, not least of which is the fact that it's packed full of unforgettable pop songs, and proves once and for all that the four lads from Australia are much more than 'just another boy band'. And despite never having written or recorded any of their own songs just two years prior to the release of the record, Luke, Michael, Calum or Ashton share a writing credit on all but one of the tracks. It's quite an achievement considering most first albums usually fall into one of two categories: in the case of many pop artists, their debut might be rapidly assembled and rushed onto the market to capitalize on a lone hit, while more serious artists often fill it with songs written several years before they were even in a position to start thinking about putting an album together. If a musician is serious about making their mark, the search for the perfect batch of introductory songs can be a long and exhaustive, but necessary, process. A balanced and well thought-out debut album is the best way for any singer or band to make a good first impression, which was always the aim for the boys.

There is no denying that 5 Seconds of Summer's self-titled issue has helped them make an unforgettable first impression just about everywhere in the world. The album peaked at Number One in the official Australia and New Zealand album charts, repeating the same feat in several European countries, and achieving Top 10 status in many more. Overall, the album claimed the number one spot on iTunes in more than seventy countries.

In the UK, the album had a tough fight, going head-to-head with Ed Sheeran's second album, *Multiply,* the much-anticipated follow-up to his multi-platinum debut, *Plus*. Sheeran's record was in its second week of release and it had already become the UK's fastest-selling album of the year so far, with the TV broadcast of his performance at the Glastonbury music festival helping keep sales extremely strong. To help bolster their own sales, the boys played a couple of intimate gigs and held signing sessions at HMV stores in Manchester and London. Limited to a couple of hundred spaces, both gigs proved to be extremely popular and demand for tickets far exceeded the capacity of the venues. Fans who had failed to get in waited patiently outside the stores, happy to chant and sing 5SOS songs. The boys were keen not to disappoint any of the unlucky ones and continued signing CDs long after the session was due to finish. In the end, it wasn't quite enough and 5 Seconds of Summer had to settle for a very respectable Number Two entry on the OCC's UK Album Chart, with sales of nearly 67,000 copies.

In the US, the album was released almost a full month after everywhere else in order to benefit from the arrival of One Direction's Where We Are Tour. Thus the 5SOS lads were available to promote the album on top-rated daytime television show *Today*, perform a mini-gig in New York's Rockefeller Plaza, and then take part in a *Jimmy Kimmel Live* 'block party', which saw the band shut down one of Los Angeles' busiest city centre streets to perform a free open-air concert for the popular late-night chat show host. The effect was to send the boys' album sales through the roof. Sailing past projected figures, the record eventually sold more than 258,000 copies in its first week and triumphantly topped the *Billboard* Top 200 Album Chart. It was good news all the way: not only had they hit Number One in the US, 5 Seconds of Summer had also delivered the year's biggest-selling debut album so far, as well as the biggest selling debut by any group since *American Idol* alumnus Chris Daughtry and his band released theirs in 2006. They may not have been the first

Australian act to score a US Number One album in 2014 – singer-songwriter Sia Furler had already done so a few weeks earlier – but they were breaking a few records of their own, becoming the first Australian act ever to enter the chart at Number One with their first album, selling more copies than any other Australian artist's debut in the process.

Having broken so many records and made so many headlines, it's worth taking a closer look at the twelve songs that make up 5 Seconds of Summer, as well as examining some of the bonus tracks that have been included on various special editions released around the world.

The album begins with what was eventually chosen to be the band's first international single, 'She Looks So Perfect'. Written by Ashton and Michael, along with Jake Sinclair, the track was also produced by Sinclair, with co-production and re-mix by Eric Valentine. Ashton describes it as being about running away with someone, leaving a boring life behind and finding new adventures with the person you love, but most people remember it simply as 'the American Apparel underwear song'. Sinclair had shown up to the writing session with the American Apparel line already in his head, but he was worried that a song about underwear might just be 'a little too weird'. Fortunately, as they explained in the song's behind the scenes YouTube video, the band 'love weird', and the line quickly became the foundation for the song's unforgettable chorus.

HMV.com described it as 'a stomping, full-bloodied,

pop-rocker, with a colossal chorus … easily the best bit of random product placement you'll hear all year'. Alter the Press! proclaimed the song 'ready and willing to be the tune of the summer', stating, 'you'll be singing along after just one listen'. Ashton revealed in the video, 'We were waiting for that perfect song to really represent us.' Luke agreed, adding, 'We just wanted to put out something [for the first record] that was different to everything else that's out there.' It was definitely mission accomplished, then, and the song became the perfect calling card for the band, neatly laying out their manifesto – big guitars, big chorus and even bigger energy.

Next up is the song that was chosen as the second single in most countries, 'Don't Stop', written by Calum and Luke, Steve Robson and Michael 'busbee' Busbee, with Robson also on production duties. In the accompanying YouTube track by track video, Ashton simply labels it as a 'party song … something you can dance to'. This was a sentiment echoed by reviewer Arianne Arciaga, who wrote in student magazine the *Chabot Spectator*, 'If you're looking for a song that will get you up on your feet and will make your head bang in the car, "Don't Stop" by 5 Seconds of Summer is the perfect song for you!' Luke describes the track's lyrics as being 'about a girl at a party that everyone wants to take home', and while those lyrics are filled with some fairly cheeky innuendo, they never push it to the point of being crass or inappropriate, with the Guardian Liberty Voice pointing out, 'The fun come-ons of lead singer Luke Hemmings add to the thrill of the number.'

While it's equally as enjoyable as 'She Looks So Perfect', with HMV calling it 'ridiculously catchy' and *Billboard* saying its chorus hook 'is the highlight of the whole album', if anything, the song's production makes it slightly looser and decidedly more punk than their previous single. With heavier riff and drums pushing it more towards the likes of Blink-182, Digital Spy noted, 'Blink-182 may have released their first song long before any of the Aussie four-piece were even born, but that hasn't deterred 5SOS from being the band's loyal understudies.'

'Good Girls' sprang to life during the December 2012 London sessions with Scouting For Girls' Roy Stride, with additional input from Josh Wilkinson – a founding member of indie rock-pop band Go:Audio – producer Feldmann and songwriting and production duo Parkhouse and Tizzard, who all share co-writing credits on the song with Ashton and Michael. In the track by track behind the scenes video for 'Good Girls', Calum relates how Stride had initially presented the basic idea for the lyric to him and Luke during their writing session, saying, 'Roy was like, "I've got this lyric – good girls are just bad girls that haven't been caught," and Luke and I were like, "You know what? This lyric suits Ash and Michael's style of writing," and thus the song passed to them the following day.

While it's true the fun, tongue-in-cheek lyrics have plenty in common with 'She Looks So Perfect', the production removes much of that song's polish and creates a quirkier and darker slice of pop-punk, with crashing guitars, synthetic singing, half-spoken and half-sung background vocals and a chanting chorus that turns it into an undisputed anthem, making it three high-tempo rock tracks in a row.

'Kiss Me Kiss Me' is the fourth entry on the album, and was written by Calum and Luke, with John Feldmann and Alex Gaskarth. It is the first of three tracks to feature a songwriting contribution from All Time Low front-man Gaskarth, and his involvement with the recording of their debut album was a particular highlight for the boys. Michael told PopCrush, 'All Time Low are basically the reason I started playing guitar and singing, so to get the opportunity to write with him, it's just insane.' Calum discussed the origins of the song, 'We wrote it about being on tour … it's a bit cheeky, this song, to be honest.' Luke elaborated: 'It's about meeting someone you really liked spending time with and not knowing if you can let it go.' Ashton explained further, saying, 'You only get so much time with the friends that you make … you move and you move and you move … this song is about making the most of the time you have with people you meet on the road.'

It is another high-tempo song, but the inclusion of some electronic beats in the middle breakdown gives this effort a more generic feel, sounding more akin to the type of pop-rock songs included on One Direction's *Midnight Memories*, such as the title track, 'Little Black Dress' and 'Little White Lies'. 'Kiss Me' has much less of the off-beat humour and lyrical mischief we've come to expect from 5 Seconds, but as a more straightforward rock song it still packs quite a punch, and certainly soars when the chorus eventually kicks in.

'18' was written by Luke and Michael, along with Richard Stannard, Seton Daunt, Ash Howes and Roy Stride. *Billboard* described '18' as 'a legitimately funny, insanely catchy ode to the frustrations of waiting for adulthood when you're still a punk kid'. It sees the 5SOS lads again putting their uniquely humorous twist on various situations, as the lyrics explore the frustrating world of fake IDs, secret tattoos and getting turned away from clubs for being underage. It was another song to come from the early sessions with Roy Stride in London, with Stannard and Rowe contributing to the sing-a-long chorus. The song is lifted from being pure pop by John Feldmann's production and some seriously heavy guitar lines. HMV described it as 'supremely catchy … [it] will have you humming the riff for days and days.'

'Everything I Didn't Say' is a song written by Ashton and Calum, with John Feldmann and Nicholas 'RAS' Furlong. RAS is an established songwriter and producer who began his career writing original music for video games before trying his hand at songwriting, and eventually signing a deal with OneRepublic's Ryan Tedder to join his Patriot Games Publishing. There he co-wrote tracks for the likes of The Wanted, Leona Lewis and *American Idol* season six winner, Jordin Sparks. His partnership with the 5 Seconds of Summer lads was extremely fruitful, producing not only 'Everything I Didn't Say', but also 'Social Casualty' and 'Independence

Day', two songs that would feature on different versions of the album available around the world. In the YouTube track by track video, Michael admits, 'Out of all the songs we have, this is the one song I wish I'd written.' Ashton explained his starting point for it: 'When you're in a relationship and then you break up and you're like, "Man, I didn't really commit to that," [it makes you realize] the other person put a lot more effort in than you did and you regret it.' Although he didn't write the song, Luke offered up his own theory about what it was about, saying, 'I think it's a cool concept ... I think it's about after a relationship's ended and you wish [you'd been] a better person in that relationship.' However, Luke was cruelly cut down by Ashton, who joked, 'We wrote it about my dog Baxter.'

A change of pace, this is the closest the album comes to a true ballad. HMV described it as having 'a proper "lights in the air" chorus', and *Billboard* commented, 'The track glows with meticulous pop production,' applauding the use of strings effects to add to the already melancholy air of the song.

'Beside You' is by far the oldest song on the album and dates back to the first writing and recording sessions the boys had, with Amy Meredith's Christian Lo Russo and Joel Chapman, in Australia in early 2012. It is the seventh entry on the album and is written by Calum, Luke and the Amy Meredith pair. The song had already been released as part of the *Somewhere New* EP, but the boys were so fond of it they thought they should re-record it and add it to their first LP. Comparing the two versions gives the clearest indication of just how far they have come in the two years since they first recorded it, and acts as a neat bridge between the band then and now.

Retaining the soulful angst in Luke's lead vocal – probably one of his best performances across the whole album – but adding subtle electronic beats and synth-string effects, it's a rousing mid-paced track, which *Billboard* thought of as 'the kind of track you'd expect to hear on a OneRepublic record, which is no bad thing if you love a good ballad'. Vaguely reminiscent of Avril Lavigne's 'I'm With You' – the power-ballad that turned her debut album, *Let Go*, into a multi-platinum international success and saw her performance on the song nominated for a Grammy Award for Best Pop Vocal – 'Beside You' acts as a reminder of the chemistry at the heart of the band and offers a first glimpse of the developing maturity and sophistication in their work. It's a fitting close for the first half of the album.

'End Up Here' was penned by Ashton and Michael, with John Feldmann and Alex Gaskarth. This song picks up the pace again, and in doing so the boys really turn up the heat, delivering yet another blistering pop-rocker. The addition of a clever keyboard-synthesizer hook with sparkling electronics bubbling under the surface produces something fresh, contemporary and radio-friendly alongside the usual mix of crashing guitars and huge, chanting choruses. With a cheeky reference to Bon Jovi's 'Living On A Prayer' and a nod to Nirvana through the mention of a Kurt Cobain T-shirt in the lyrics, it somehow manages to sound both modern and retro at the same time.

Ashton recalled in the behind the scenes YouTube video that his overriding memory of the song was 'John [Feldmann] taking off his shirt and dancing in the studio'. He explained the song was written with the live experience very much in mind: 'We needed a song that lifts the crowd ... a party song ... We wanted to write something up-tempo that gets the crowd jumping.' *Billboard* described it as 'another rollicking standout ... when the last chorus hits with handclaps instead of drums, the listener is obliged to clap right along'. HMV.com proclaimed the track as 'the album's highlight' and issued the ultimate compliment, saying, 'it sounds like the kind of track Blink-182 would have happily put their name to in the early 2000s, it's brilliant.'

'Long Way Home' is song number nine and was again written by Ashton and Michael, John Feldmann and Alex Gaskarth. Put together during Ashton and Michael's first meeting with their All Time Low hero, it was completed a mere twenty-four hours after Luke and Calum had written 'Kiss Me Kiss Me' with him during their first session. Luke summed up their relationship with the prolific Gaskarth by simply stating, 'He definitely got us.' Ashton explained just how quickly the song seemed to flow, admitting, 'It was within fifteen minutes of getting there, we had this chorus idea.' A hugely productive relationship, the boys believed their writing styles had clicked so instantly due to the musical influences they shared with Gaskarth, as well as all the 5SOS lads having grown up listening to All Time Low and learning the basics of writing and song structure from their albums.

With a lyrical shout-out to Green Day, this slightly more laid-back track, with its stuttering drum beat and driving piano hook, brings to mind 'I Miss You' by Blink-182 and sits neatly alongside some of the more radio-friendly American rock acts the boys cite as their influences. HMV wrote it was 'a little bit Jimmy Eats World, a little Good Charlotte, even a bit R.E.M.' A song of eclectic influences indeed.

'Heartbreak Girl' is written by Calum and Luke, Steve Robson and Lindy Robbins. It is another track that survives from the band's earliest writing and recording sessions, having been conceived during their first trip to London, and it eventually premiered as a free download in early 2013. For its inclusion on *5 Seconds of Summer* it is given a slight re-mix and an added layer of gloss. Luke remembers the first session with Robson, saying in their YouTube video, 'We wrote four songs and I actually didn't like ['Heartbreak Girl'] that much out of the four songs, but everyone was saying, "That song's really good."'

The track's other co-writer, LA-based Lindy Robbins, is most famous for having written Demi Lovato's 'Skyscraper' (also a Number-One hit in the UK for *X Factor*'s 2013 winner Sam Bailey) and has over twenty-five years' experience in the music industry working with a host of acts including Backstreet Boys, Selena Gomez, Leona Lewis and One Direction. Ashton revealed the special place this particular song holds in the boys' hearts: 'It's good to see the crowd singing every single word of this song, it's cool 'cos it means a lot to us as it [symbolizes] the first steps we took with coming over to the UK.' Undoubtedly the most out-and-out pop song on the album, with its simple 'boy meets girl, girl ignores boy' story told over a sleek and shiny production, it is dominated by a spiky guitar riff and some great harmonies from the boys.

'Lost Boy' is a Calum, Luke, Jarrad Rogers and Roy Stride number. Along with 'Good Girls' and '18', this is another early song that started out during the boys' sessions with Scouting For Girls' main man, Stride, and was later whipped into shape by Jarrad Rogers. Rogers is an Australian-born songwriter and producer with more than a decade's experience working with a wide variety of pop and rock artists. At the start of his career, he co-wrote with many high-profile Australian acts including Delta Goodrem and *Australian Idol* winner Guy Sebastian, before moving to his base in London. Making frequent trips to the US, Rogers now counts such mainstream international artists as Lana Del Rey, Alex Clare, Demi Lovato and Foxes among his numerous clients.

The track begins with an intentionally untidy, clattering drum intro, which gives way to a majestic, towering rock song built on super-sized guitar riffs and a soaring chorus, and delivers the clearest link to the band's heavier rock influences. It is a real highlight for the 5SOS fans who prefer to read about them in *Kerrang!* rather than catching them supporting One Direction on tour. While this song is included as track eleven on the Australian and New Zealand standard versions of the album, it is replaced on the UK edition by 'English Love Affair' and in the US by 'Mrs All American', undoubtedly to appeal more to these markets.

'English Love Affair' is written by Ashton and Michael, with Rick Parkhouse, George Tizzard, Roy Stride and Josh Wilkinson also receiving co-writing credits. Yet another track with its origins in the 2012 London sessions, it was perhaps rather fittingly added to the UK version of the album, given its title and concept. Ashton came up with the basic idea for the chorus as the lads were driving to a writing session in the English seaside town of Bournemouth, quickly taking shape and referencing the chants he'd heard the crowds sing during soccer matches. Ashton recalled how the song sat on the shelf for some time, but that it brought back some good memories of their time in London: 'It was really cool and we had a great time writing it. We've recorded it since and it's the dance track on the album.'

'Mrs All American' is a Calum, Michael, Steve Robson and Ross Golan effort, and acts as a very special thank you to 5 Seconds' growing American fan base. It was a track started off by Steve Robson and subsequently completed with the help of an established songwriter in the US, Ross

Golan. Golan is yet another associate of OneRepublic's Ryan Tedder, who has penned hits for Justin Bieber, Flo Rida, Shakira, Enrique Iglesias, Maroon 5, Nicki Minaj and Lady Antebellum. With its nagging, whistling hook, eccentric percussion and peculiar screeching synth-lines, this is definitely one on which the 5SOS boys have some fun. This doesn't go unnoticed in *Billboard*'s review, as they state, 'The band's inner playfulness is on full display here, as the guys try their best to pound their chests without losing their geeky charm.'

'Amnesia' was chosen as the third official single from the album and was written by Benjamin Madden, Joel Madden, Louis Biancaniello, Michael Biancaniello and Sam Watters. It is unique in that it is the only song included on the standard twelve-track edition of the album that does not have a writing credit for any of the 5 Seconds of Summer band members. It does, however, see the boys fulfilling their lifelong dream of working with their musical heroes, Good Charlotte siblings Benji and Joel Madden. In the track by track video, the boys recalled hearing the song for the first time, Luke revealing, '[Joel and Benji] wrote it a while ago and couldn't find anyone it suited.' Michael confirmed, 'They were saving it for "The Special People".' Strangely, none of the 5SOS lads seemed particularly impressed with it initially, but they later told how they had grown to realize what an incredibly powerful song it was: 'It's really heartfelt ... it's very special to us as a band.' It is without a doubt the most surprising and sophisticated track on the album, a fact acknowledged by *Billboard*, praising its 'affecting vocal performance and the most searing lyrics on the album … Taking older listeners back to the relative heartache of dissolving high school romance'. The magazine proclaimed, '"Amnesia" demonstrates the versatility of 5SOS.' As the album closes, it is refreshingly downbeat. HMV labelled it 'quiet and sweet … a sombre bookend'. And there's no denying that this tender hint of sadness packs more of an emotional punch coming as it does at the end of an otherwise upbeat collection of songs. Containing deeply profound lyrics sung with unexpectedly raw emotion over a delicate acoustic guitar and drenched in sweeping strings, the final ballad is the unmistakable high point of the album and the song that's certain to win the band a legion of new admirers.

In the UK, the deluxe edition of the album contains three bonus tracks, 'Social Casualty', 'Never Be' and 'Voodoo Doll'. The first song was written by Luke and Michael, John Feldmann and Nicholas 'RAS' Furlong. Originating in the same writing sessions as 'Everything I Didn't Say', this song is by far the most clearly influenced by early Blink-182, exposing the band's pop-punk roots. The lyrics are overflowing with teenage rebelliousness and the guitar riffs are big, loud and pushed front and centre in the final mix. It is certainly worthy of a band who could more aptly support Green Day than One Direction on tour.

'Never Be' was written by all four members of the band,

along with John Feldmann. Another slow song, with hints of Green Day's 'Wake Me Up When September Ends', it tells the story of two discontented teenagers, hopelessly in love, who wish they could stay young forever, run away from their hometown and escape the inevitable future they see mapped out for them. It all adds up to a sweet and poignant song, with a strong vocal performance from the boys and an unexpected subtlety in its delivery.

'Voodoo Doll' is a song written by Ashton, Calum and UK-based songwriters Adam Argyle and Fiona Bevan, and survived from some of the boys' earliest writing and recording sessions. Argyle has more than a decade's experience writing with some of the UK's biggest pop artists, including Will Young, Pixie Lott and Olly Murs, and specializes in finding, nurturing and developing the talents of new singer-songwriters, as he has done with Newton Faulkner and Gabrielle Aplin. Bevan is an artist in her own right and gained massive exposure as a songwriter when a track she had written years earlier with a then unknown Ed Sheeran, 'Little Things', became a worldwide smash for One Direction in 2012. 'Voodoo Doll' tells the tale of someone so uncontrollably in love that they feel they must be living under some sort of supernatural spell. It is contained in a fairly straightforward pop-rock song, with chiming guitar riffs and thundering drums, topped off with some sweeping synth-strings, and is a welcome addition as a bonus track for any fan.

The iTunes deluxe edition contains the exclusive bonus track, 'Greenlight'. This song is written by Ashton and Michael, with the aid of Steve Robson and James Bourne, chief writer for Busted. Written in London in 2012, it is a pure adrenalin rush of a song, with lusty lyrics and screeching guitar feedback, it delivers one of the 'punkiest' moments in their extensive songbook.

Alongside four different versions of the cover art for Target, the US retailer had an exclusive edition of the album containing no fewer than four bonus tracks. 'Tomorrow Never Dies' was written by Ashton and Calum, Brittany Burton and John Feldmann. Certainly the most unusual track the boys have released to date, with heavy electronic effects throughout and chanting backing vocals, it has more in common with *Hybrid Theory*-era Linkin Park and Depeche Mode's *Violator* than their usual pop-punk influences.

'Independence Day', written by Ashton, Calum, Feldmann and Furlong, is a driving pop-rock track that benefits hugely from its crashing guitar riff, stuttering vocal effects and an unforgettable sing-a-long chorus.

'Close As Strangers', also written by Ashton and Michael, as well as Roy Stride, Rick Parkhouse and George Tizzard, is another heartfelt ballad about being on the road and missing home, given a shimmering, summery production and uplifting chorus that wouldn't sound out of place in a Backstreet Boys song.

'Out of My Limit', written by Calum and Luke, is one of the

boys' earliest recordings, and is lifted from the *Somewhere New* EP. Rough and ready, with super-sweet harmonies, sitting next to their newer recordings it neatly shows the transition 5 Seconds of Summer have made in such a short time.

The JB Hi-Fi edition contains the bonus tracks 'Wrapped Around Your Finger', written by Luke and Michael, with John Feldmann, and 'Pizza'. This rather different song, with its ambient electronics and chiming guitar solo, has an air of Snow Patrol's 'Chasing Cars' or recent Coldplay work, perhaps giving an indication of their future development as a band. 'Pizza', written by all four members of the band, is a thirty-eight-second ode to the joys of pizza slices, and was a hidden track on the cassette single version of 'She Looks So Perfect', which was released as a very special limited edition for UK Record Store Day 2014.

For a relatively new band, they have created an impressive library of songs that successfully encompass a number of sub-genres, as demonstrated by the range of tracks on the various international editions of *5 Seconds of Summer*. It is of great interest to both fans and observers of the music industry as to where the boys decide to take their sound in the future.

CHAPTER SIXTEEN

DON'T STOP

'Whoever the biggest acts in the world are, whether that's One Direction, Rihanna or Bruno Mars, it's our ambition to be spoken about alongside those, with equal status.'
NICK RAPHAEL, PRESIDENT OF CAPITOL RECORDS
UK, *MUSIC WEEK*

O pinion may still be divided on 5 Seconds of Summer's position in the music world – many rock purists simply can't see past their association with One Direction and dismiss them as 'too pop', while the boys' insistence that they are a 'real band', with a majority share in making their own music, may alienate some of their younger fans who have no interest in the band's desire for creative freedom and simply want to swoon over their posters and scream at their concerts – the fact is, they have made their mark and are undoubtedly here to stay.

Talking to *Billboard* magazine in August 2014, 5 Seconds drummer Ashton Irwin was quick to reassure fans that his band had no intention of giving up their fight to convert the doubters. 'Some people think "Oh, they're just another boy band. They'll have a thing and then disappear." But we're challenging that thought.' He continued, 'We're so proud of the music we make – we love it – and we're fearless. If anyone puts us down, we don't care. Isn't that somewhat punk – not giving a damn what people say?' Whatever people think about their music, the attitude the boys share is one that will help see them go the distance.

With the incredible global success of their debut album, and no let-up in their busy touring schedule in sight, it looks like the breakthrough 5SOS had in 2014 may simply go down as the first tiny step in their incredible journey, rather than the crowning glory of all their extraordinary achievements so far. With thousands of new fans joining the 5SOS family every day, Luke, Michael, Calum and Ashton should cancel any plans to take it easy – they're set to be incredibly busy for the foreseeable future. If the boys are to maintain the momentum they've built up in 2014, it looks like they will have to cut back on those trips to Nando's, as there's a lot of hard work to be done.

Aside from performances at the Video Music Awards on 24 August 2014 – where the boys won the Best Lyric Video for 'Don't Stop' – and the iTunes Festival in London on 4 September, the next major event in the 5SOS calendar was the release of 'Amnesia' as the third official single from *5 Seconds of Summer*. The song was the band's secret weapon and was set to help the album cross over even further into the mainstream.

The lyric video was released towards the beginning of July, featuring stark black and white photography and moody shots of the boys' faces, with the lyrics of the track projected onto them – simple and strikingly effective. It used hundreds of visual reminders of the boys and their journey so far, from early snapshots and concert wristbands to penguins, pineapples and games consoles.

When the official video was eventually revealed on 31 July, it was in direct contrast to the previous one, bursting with colour and bathed in a glowing, late-summer light. With a beautifully nostalgic collage of images, it shows the lads returning to their hometown and hanging out with friends. Also featuring a nod to the time they spent practising in their garages at home, the scenes perfectly sum up the song's heartfelt lyrics. Within a couple of weeks the video had passed six-and-a-half million views on YouTube, proving to be one of the boys' most popular clips to date.

While not as successful as its two predecessors, 'Amnesia' nevertheless entered the Top 20 in the US, Canada and New Zealand, and peaked at Number Seven in Australia, proving there was no let-up in people's desire for 5 Seconds of Summer's music.

As far back as the first week of July 2014, the boys had already unveiled their plans for the Rock Out With Your Socks

Out Tour in 2015, which would see them playing their first European headline dates. They would visit twenty-six arenas, taking them to eleven different countries in mainland Europe throughout May. Thirteen more dates in the UK were added, finishing with two nights at Wembley's SSE Arena in June. They would then fly to Australia to play their first ever headline arena dates on their home soil on a five-night tour. Within a week of that announcement, unwilling to stop the news rolling in, the lads revealed to their US fans that the roadshow would carry on to America, stopping in more than twenty states as it travelled around the country in July and August, before coming to an end in Palm Beach, Florida on 13 September.

If there were still any doubts about 5 Seconds of Summer's ability to emerge from the shadow of their former tour mates, they were quickly blown away by the speed at which the dates began to sell out. It may well be a case of 'One Direction who?' as the boys finally get the chance to show everyone exactly what they are capable of: playing a full set, consisting of their own songs, to a crowd who they know have all come along just to see them in action. Anyone worrying about how these shows might differ from the support slot gigs should take comfort in Ashton's insistence that the band were looking to their greatest heroes, Green Day, for pointers. He told *Alternative Press*, 'I love that [Green Day's Billie Joe Armstrong] can command a stadium. He and [Foo Fighters'] Dave Grohl have that power. I look at that and get really inspired. That's the way we perform, a lot of yelling.' As 20,000 people sing along to 'Don't Stop',

'She Looks So Perfect' and 'Amnesia', repeating every word at the top of their voices, there will be no one in these crowds left wondering about who is looking to take over as the rightful heirs to the One Direction throne.

The financial rewards associated with selling millions of records and playing to packed arenas on international tours are also tantalizingly close – the five members of One Direction were set to earn an estimated $23 million each in 2014 – and with the added bonus of 5 Seconds of Summer writing virtually all of their own songs, it seems money might not be something Luke, Michael, Calum and Ashton will need to worry about for a long time. While Michael admitted the band have yet to enjoy much of the income made from their record sales, telling the *Daily Telegraph* the band's bank balance 'hasn't really changed', their long-term financial security was no longer an issue.

With much of their time in 2015 already spoken for, it's hard to imagine when the boys will have time to write and record their already eagerly anticipated second album. Everyone lucky enough to have tickets for upcoming 5 Seconds gigs will undoubtedly already have their fingers crossed for a sneak preview of a new song or two. It seems unlikely they will follow 1D's four albums in four years release pattern, a difficult schedule to maintain when the band members themselves are writing and playing all their own music. Reassuringly, it looks as though their UK label boss, Nick Raphael, is willing to give the boys the time to get it right, as he stated in *Music Week*, 'We have to make sure that the next album is full of brilliant songs.' Discussing the eventual release of album number two, he revealed he has high hopes for the band's immediate future: 'I want [5SOS] to be a real act that when a release date is set, everyone else wants to move out of the way because they know a big record is coming . . . That's the ambition and we hope that we're at the beginning of a career. The band are good enough, the management are seasoned enough – they're as good as you get.'

We can only speculate as to where the next album will take them, as they delve even deeper into their musical influences, mature as songwriters and grow more proficient as musicians. Are we likely to see the boys finally collaborating with their One Direction tour mates, or can we expect something considerably less pop from the boys from Down Under? They have already revealed their ambitions to be seen as real rock musicians, embraced fully by their peers in the wider rock community, so is a full rock album completely out of the question? Perhaps they will manage to snag writing sessions with even more of their music idols. Who wouldn't want to hear the songs that might result from sessions where the boys managed to sit down to write with Green Day's Billie Joe Armstrong, Pete Wentz of Fall Out Boy or Foo Fighters' front man, Dave Grohl?

There is also the question of what they intend to do with their own label, Hi or Hey Records. Set up with the understanding that the boys would be looking to find a few new singers or young bands who might otherwise struggle to get a foothold on the first rung of the music industry ladder, it may only be a matter of time before they discover the next Blink-182, All Time Low or Paramore. Luke even told *Billboard* in August 2014, 'A girl version of us would be cool.'

The 5 Seconds of Summer story may have only just begun, and while the band's future impact on the music scene may be far from decided, through their own records and the bands they may sign in the future, it's safe to say they have made a lasting impression. In the space of just three years, they have amassed millions of fans around the world, and while the jury is still out among some of their harshest critics on their place in the musical landscape, one thing is for sure: as far as the boys' mission to bring pop-punk to the masses is concerned, they have achieved a resounding success. 'Just to have guitars on the radio again is nice,' confessed spokesman Ashton. He hoped the band's true legacy would have a much greater, more far-reaching effect, though: 'If a kid picks up drumsticks because of our band, job done.' Michael was even more emphatic about it as he tweeted his followers, 'I want people to be still wearing our shirts in thirty years' time.'

The only certainty is that whatever they produce, and whenever they decide to let the rest of the world hear the fruits of their labours, there will be millions of fans eagerly waiting to embrace their new songs, sing along at their concerts and help them to continue on their triumphant journey, taking on the world as they go.

SOURCES

NEWSPAPERS AND MAGAZINES

Alternative Press
Billboard
Classic Pop
Daily Mail
Daily Star
Guardian
Girlfriend
Hollywood Reporter
Kerrang!
Music Week
Rock Sound
Rolling Stone
Rouse Hill Times
Sydney Morning Herald
Teen Vogue
(Sydney) Daily Telegraph
Sun
Sun-Herald
Top Of The Pops

BOOKS

She Looks So Perfect – Mary Boone
The Guinness Book of British Hit Singles and Albums

TELEVISION and RADIO

2day FM 104.1 Sydney
60 Minutes
9.65 TIC FM
AwesomenessTV
Capital FM
Extra
KIIS 1065 Radio
MTV
Nova FM
Singapore Radio
Sunday Brunch
The Late Late Show
Today Show
WPLW North Carolina

WEBSITES

5SOS.com

Annandalehotel.com

ARIAcharts.com

Ask.fm

Alterthepress.com

Billboard.com

Capitalfm.com

Thechabotspectator.com

Coupdemainmagazine.com

Facebook.com

Fuseonline.org.uk

Gibson.com

Guardianlv.com

HMV.com

Hollywoodlife.com

Instagram.com

Modestmanagement.com

Musicnetwork.ie

Musicfeeds.com

Musictakeabow.com

News.com.au

Norwest.nsw.edu.au

Officialcharts.com

Popcrush.com

Punktastic.com

Seventeen.com

Sonyatv.com

Startupsmart.au

Sugarscape.com

Tellymix.co.uk

Theaustralian.com.au

Thehillsarealive.com.au

Thehothits.com

USAtoday.com

Vevo.com

Wondermgmt.com

YouTube.com

PICTURE ACKNOWLEDGEMENTS

Page 1: Astrid Stawiarz / Getty Images (top left); Don Arnold / Getty Images (top right); John Lamparski / Getty Images (bottom left); Mark Robert Milan / FilmMagic / Getty Images (bottom right)

Page 2: REX / AGF s.r.l. (both)

Page 3: Turgeon-Steffman / Splash News (top); Splash News (bottom)

Page 4: REX / David Fisher (top); REX / Broadimage (bottom)

Page 5: Redferns via Getty Images (top); Cindy Ord / Getty Images for SiriusXM (bottom)

Page 6: Mark Metcalfe / Getty Images (top left & bottom right); REX / Broadimage (top right); Kevin Mazur / WireImage / Getty Images (bottom left)

Page 7: Suzan / EMPICS / PA Images (all)

Page 8: REX / AGF s.r.l. (top); Michael Tran / FilmMagic / Getty Images (bottom)

INDEX

5 Seconds of Summer: Test Your Super-Fan Status

£4.99   978-1-78055-336-8